100 Flowers

This Book Belongs to:

_____

_____

_____

DADAMerra©

© 2020 DADAMERRA ALL RIGHTS RESERVED

NO PART OF THIS BOOK MAY BE REPRODUCED, STORED IN A RETRIEVAL SYSTEM, STORED IN A DATABASE AND / OR PUBLISHED IN ANY FORM OR BY ANY MEANS, ELECTRONIC, MECHANICAL, PHOTOCOPYING, RECORDING OR OTHERWISE, WITHOUT THE PRIOR WRITTEN PERMISSION OF THE PUBLISHER.

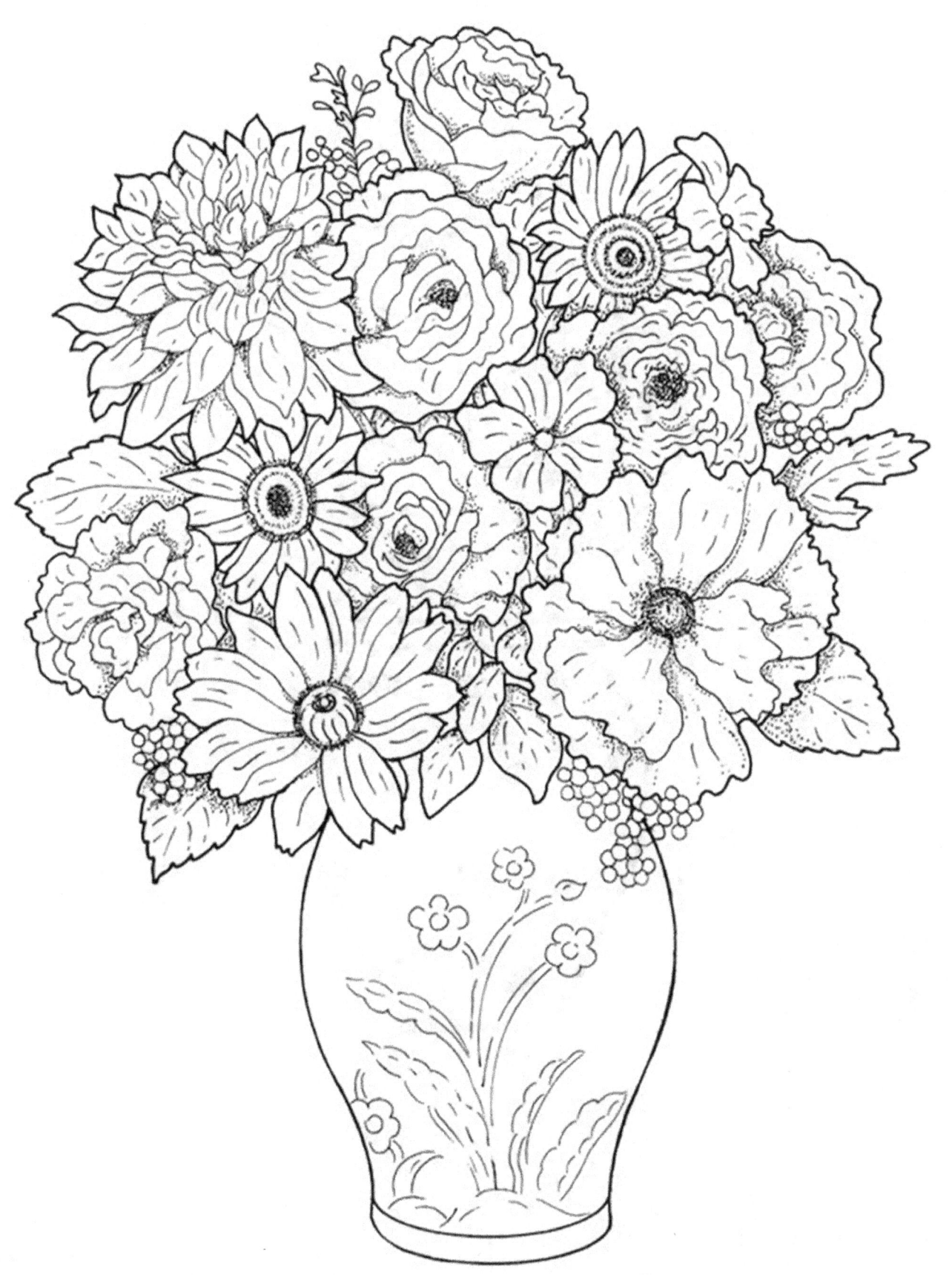

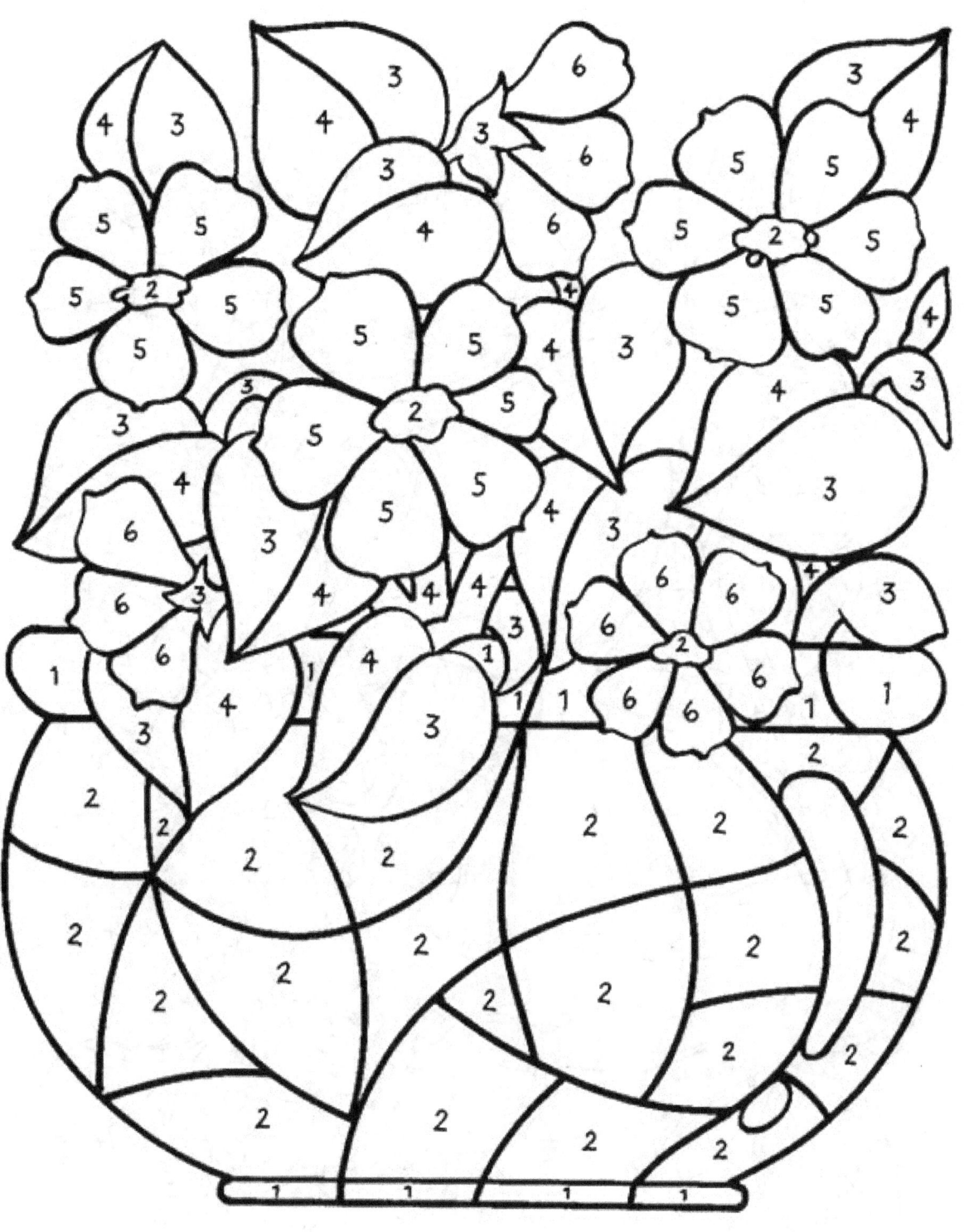

1. Red 2. Yellow 3. Light Green 4. Dark Green 5. Blue 6. Purple

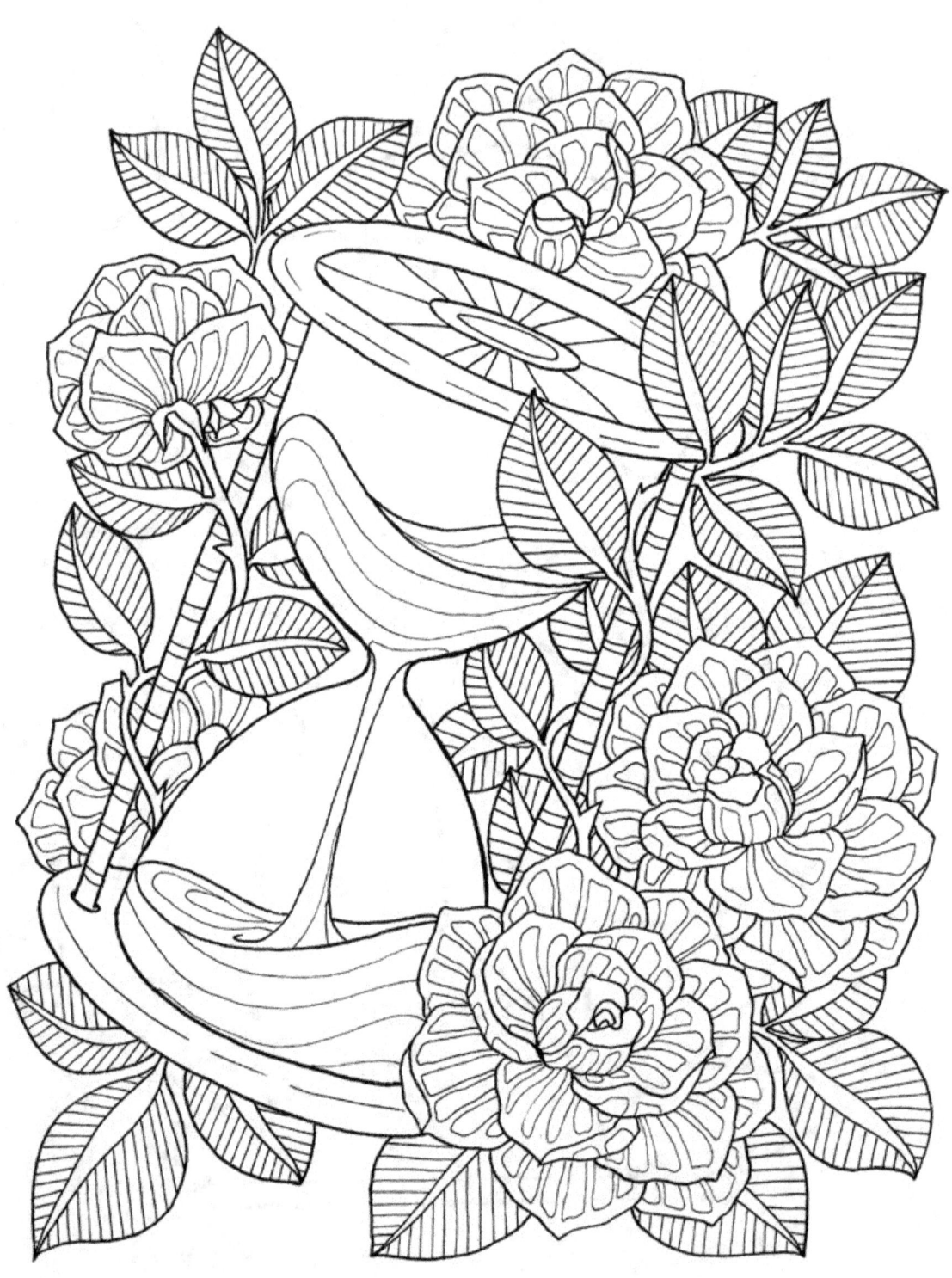

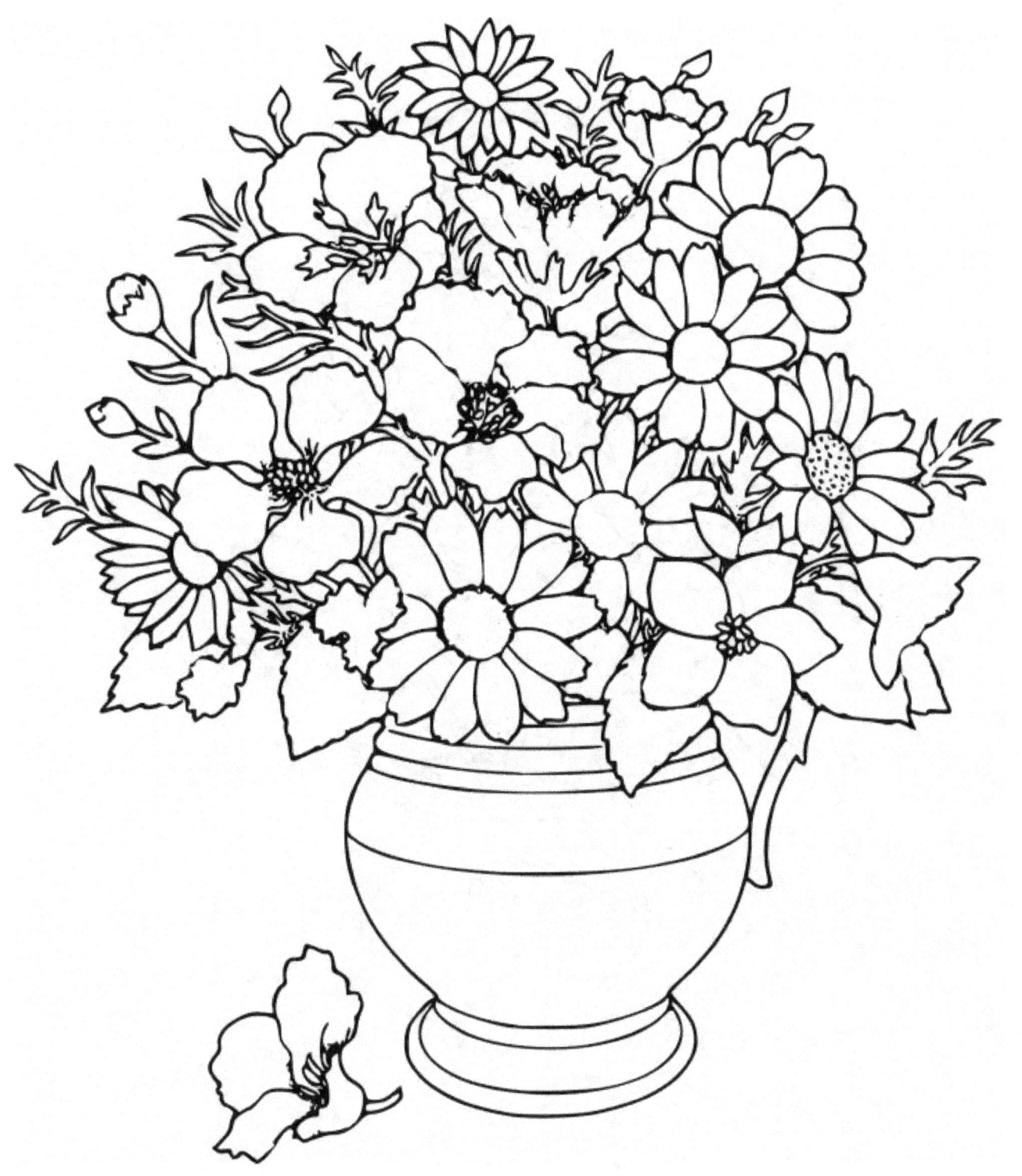

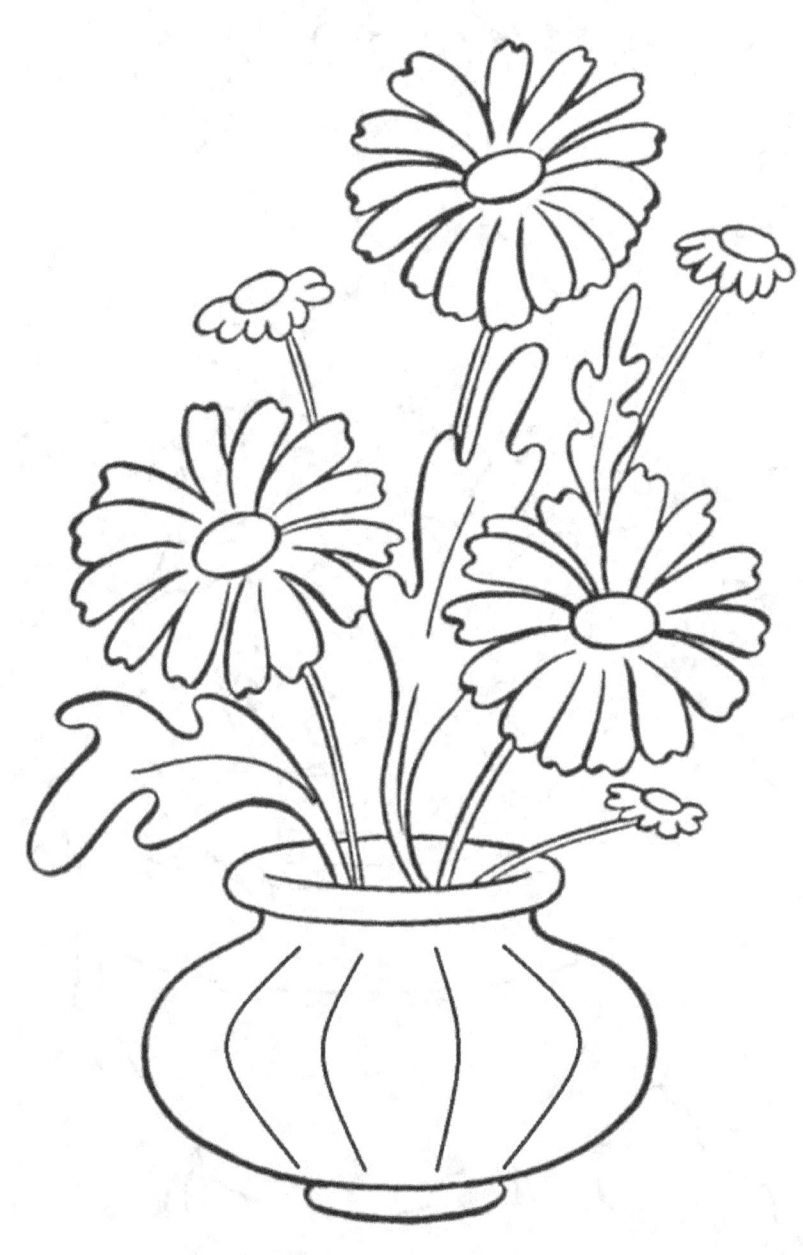

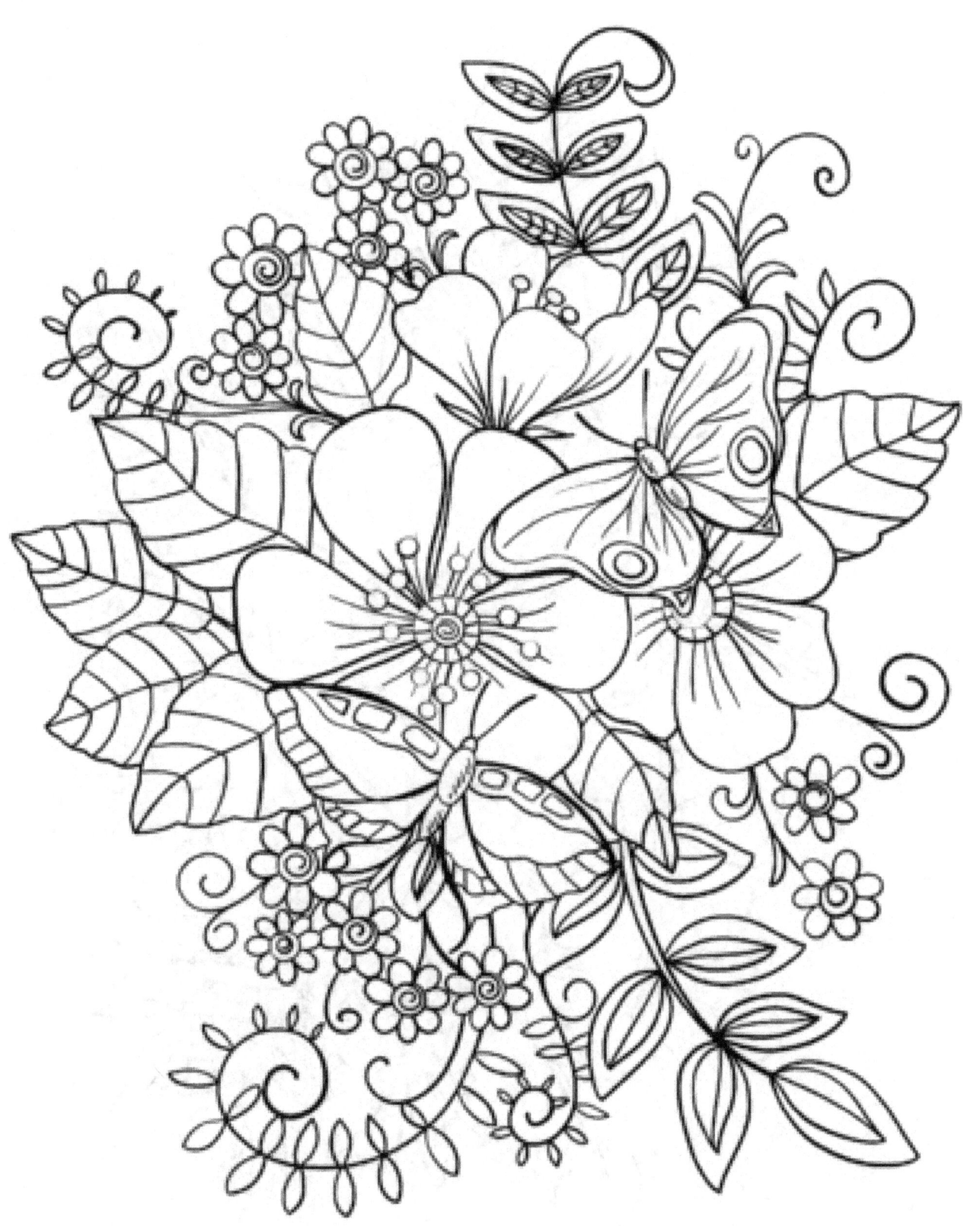

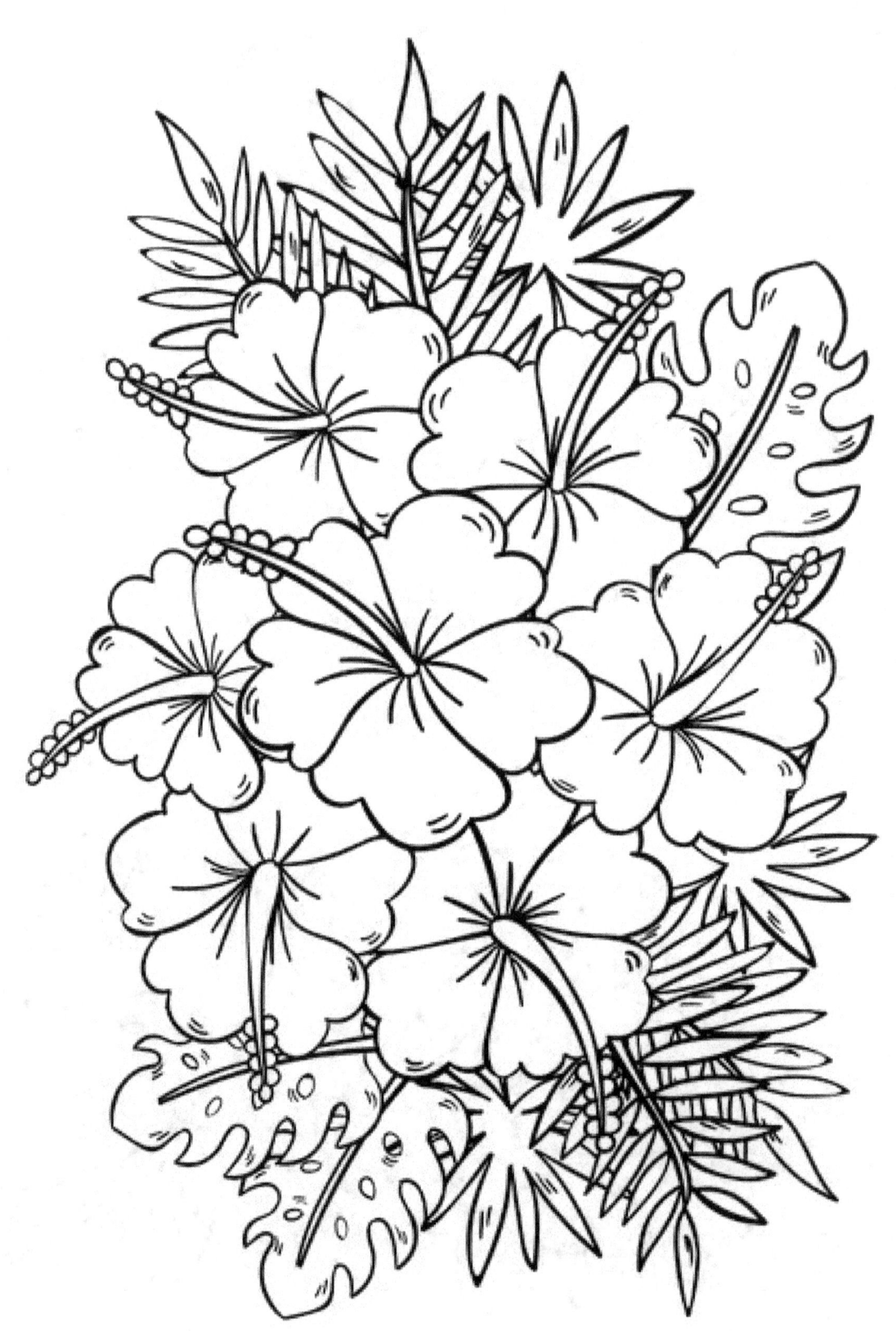

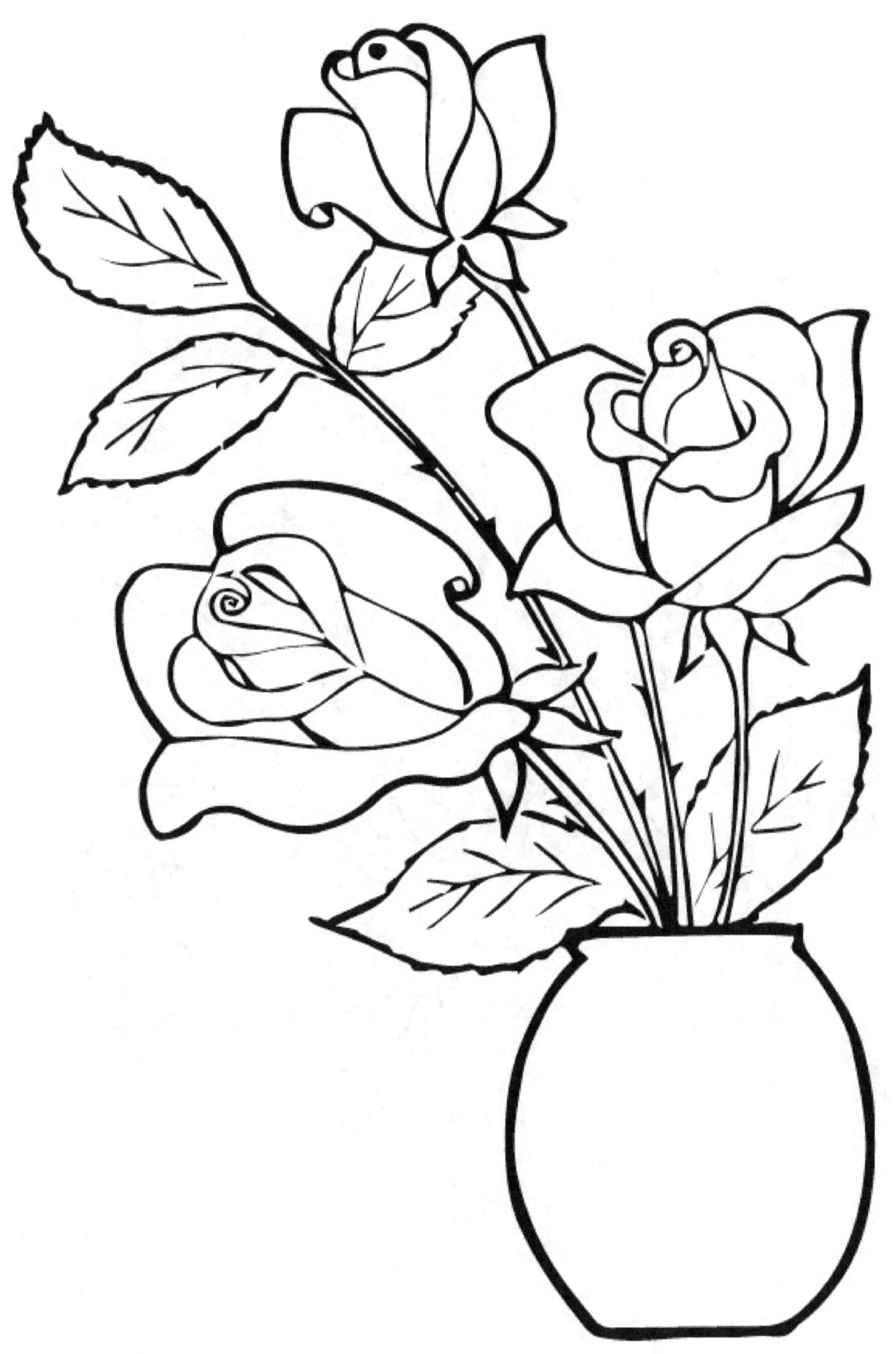

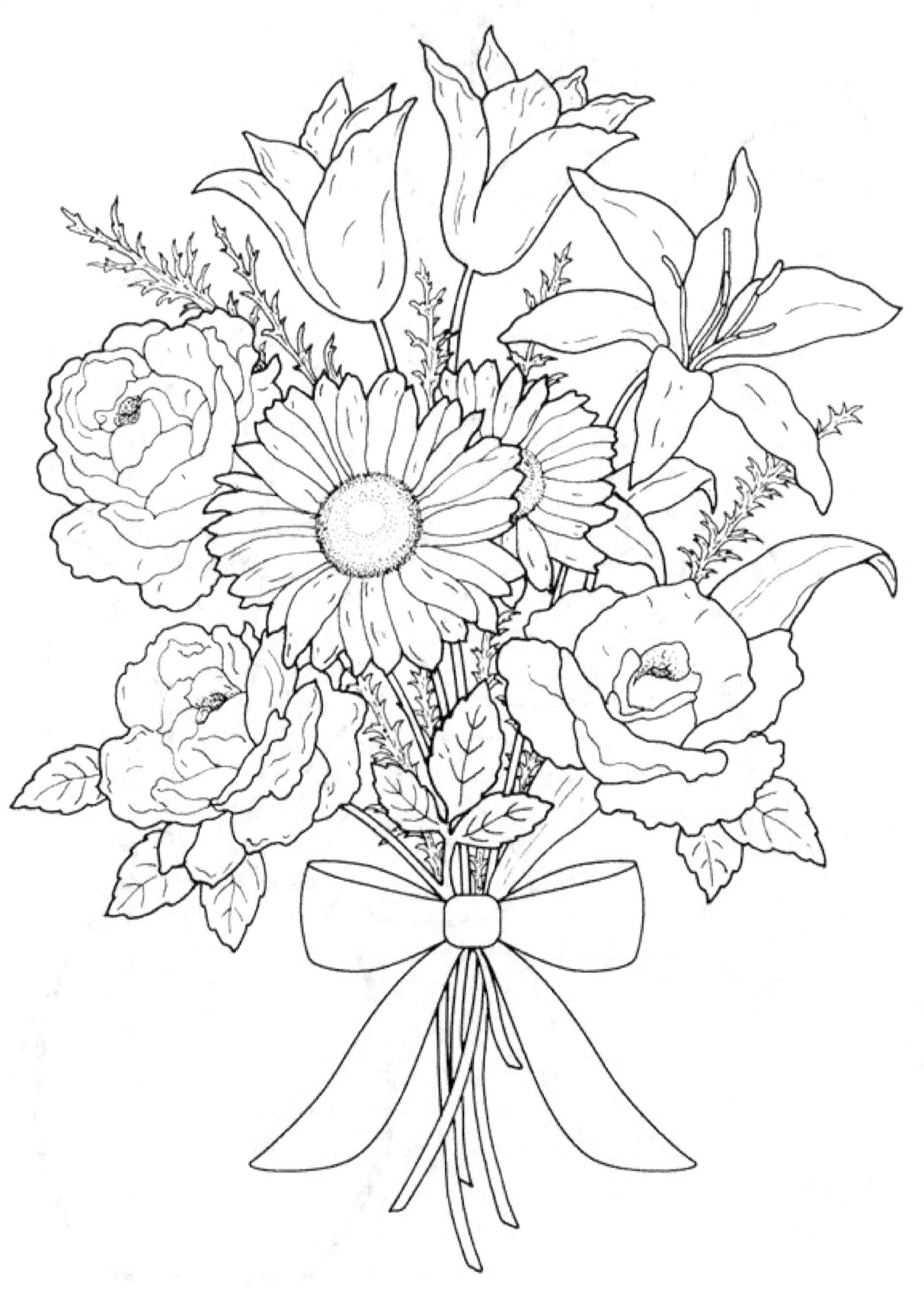

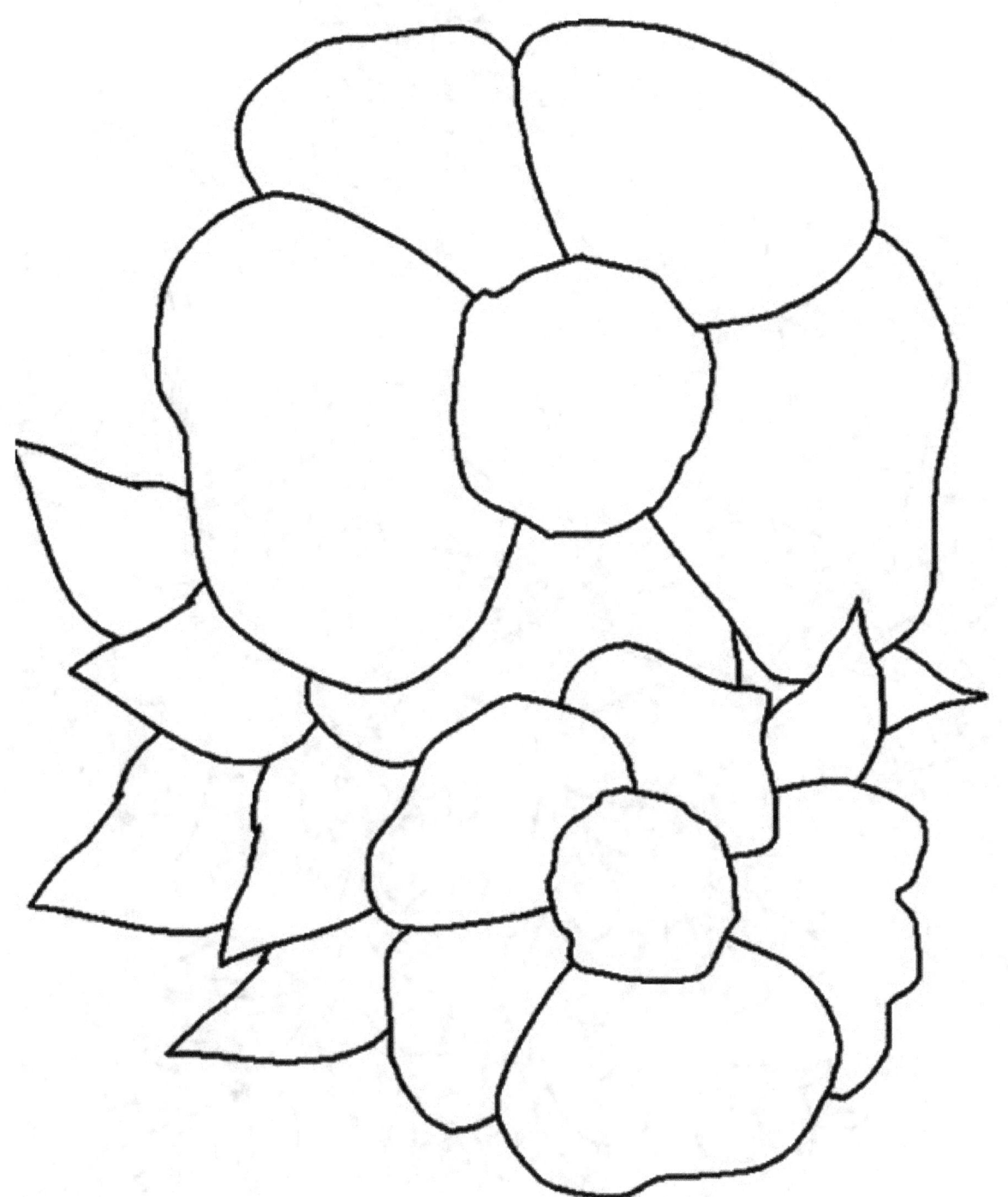

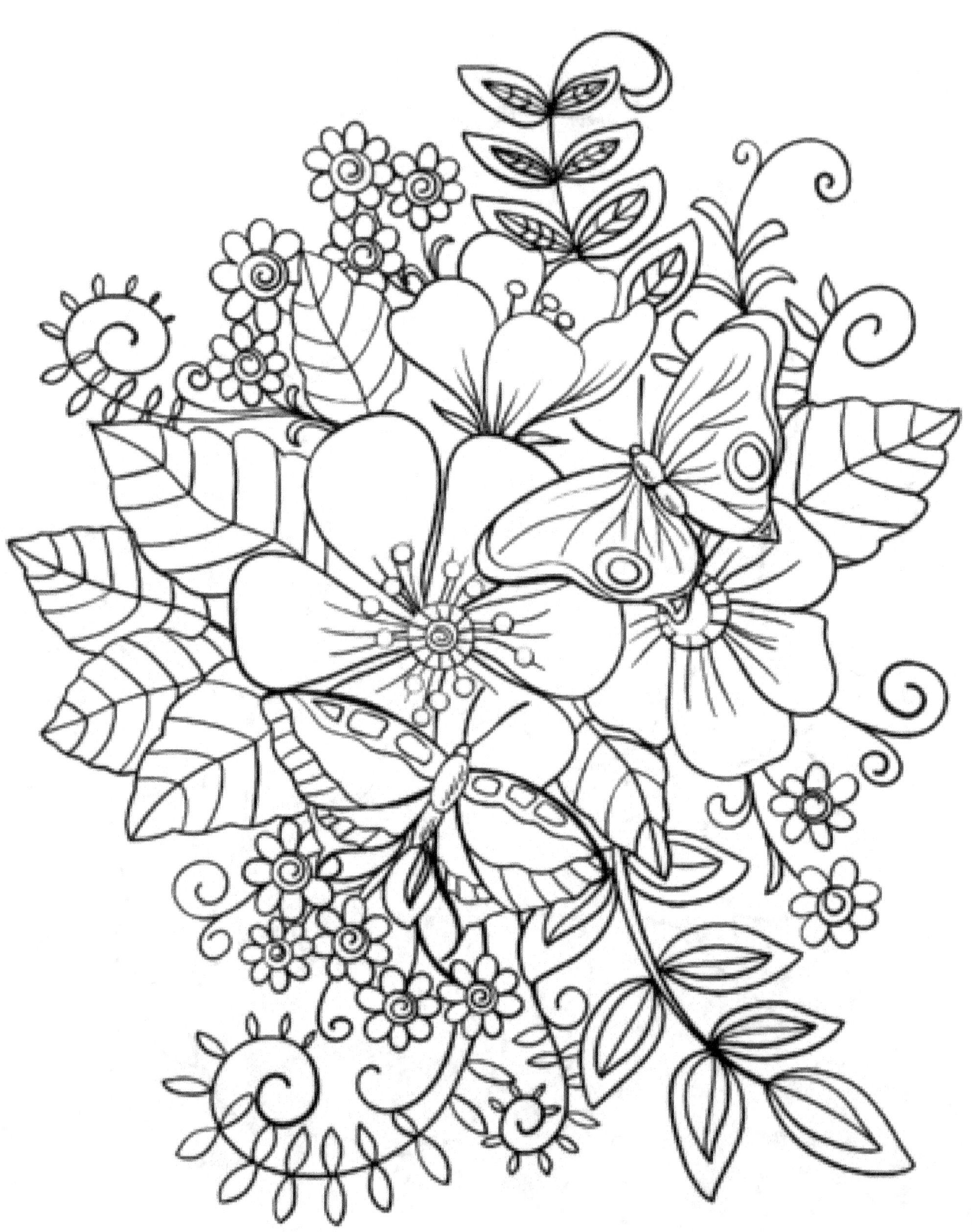

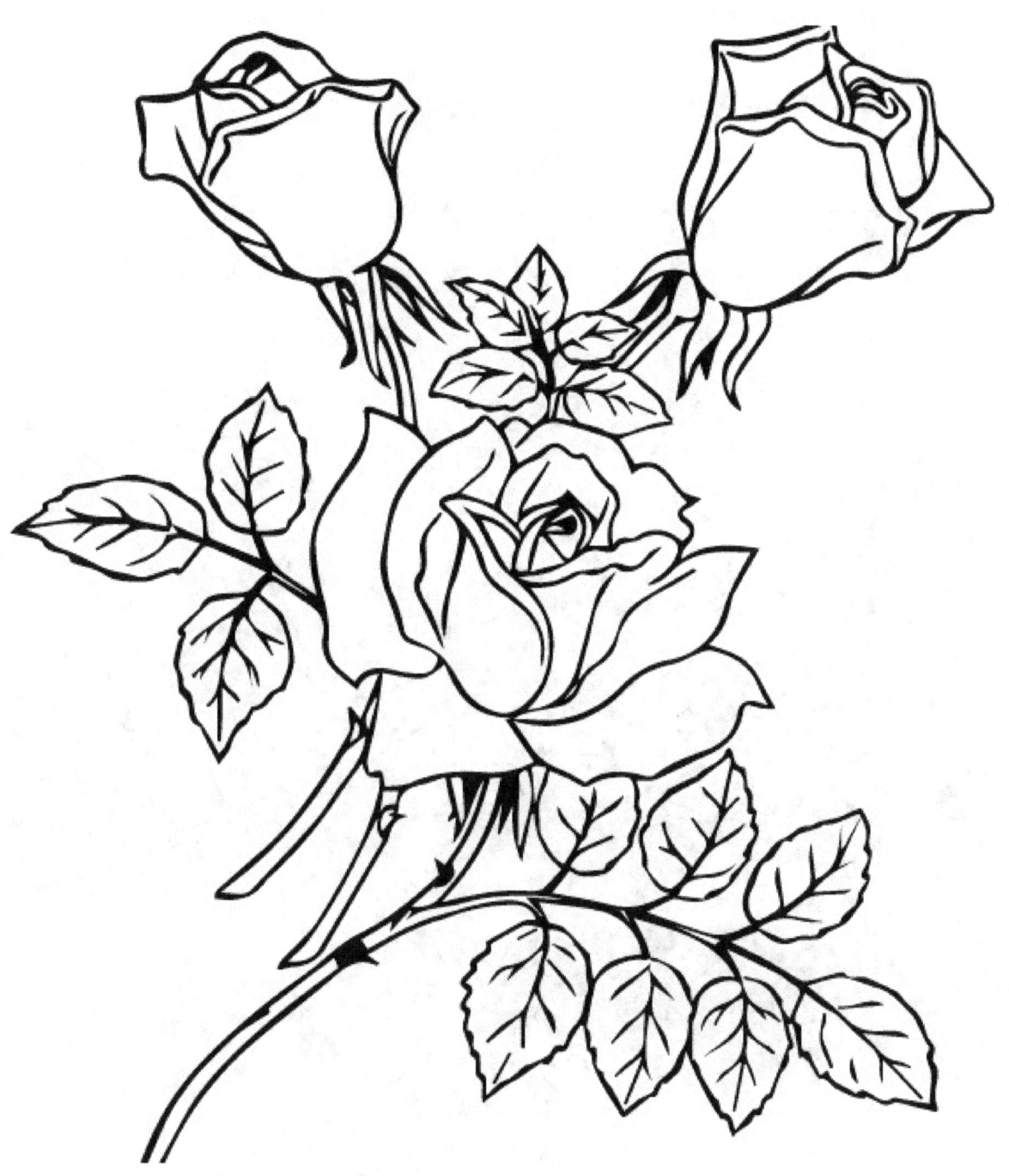

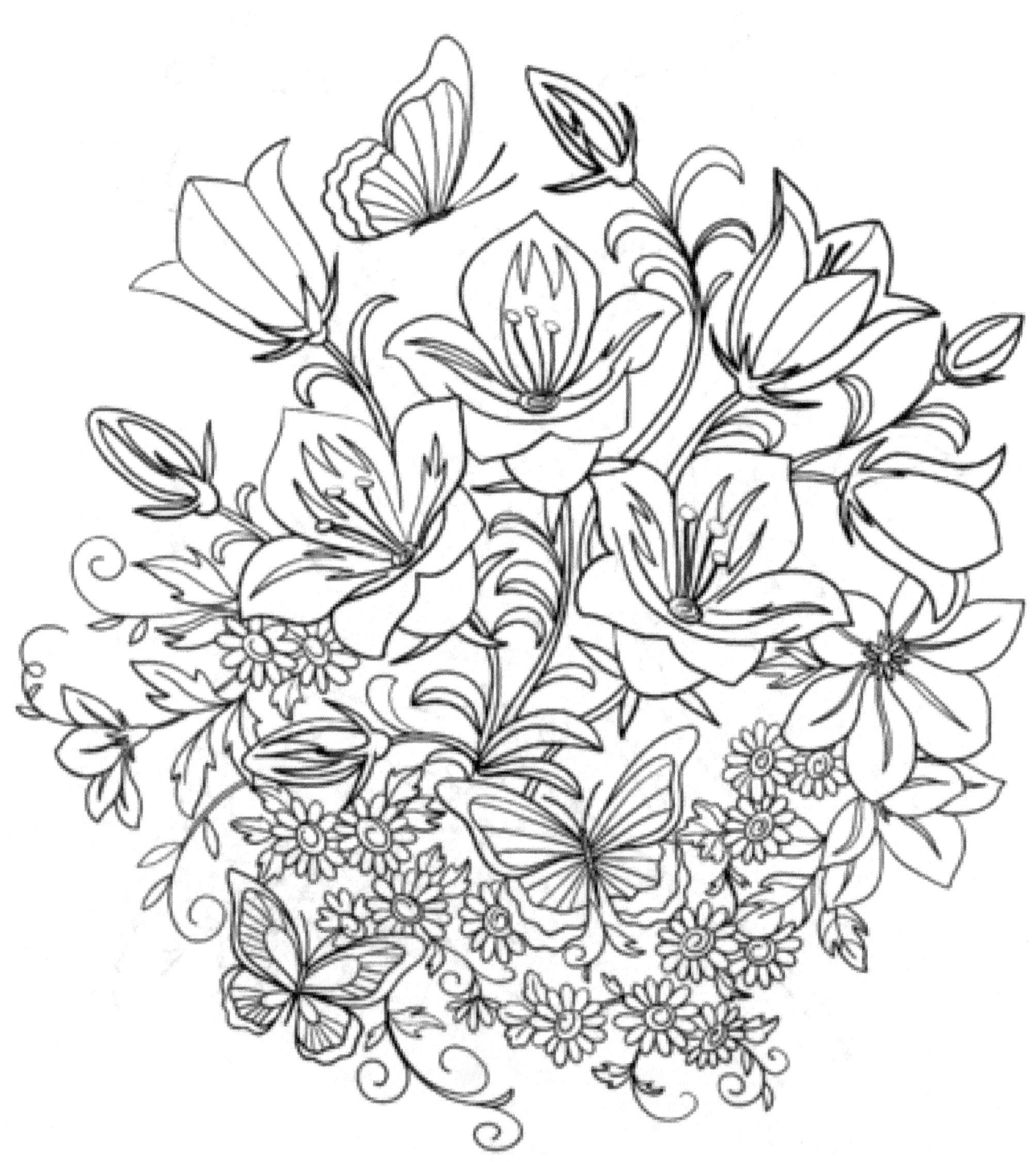

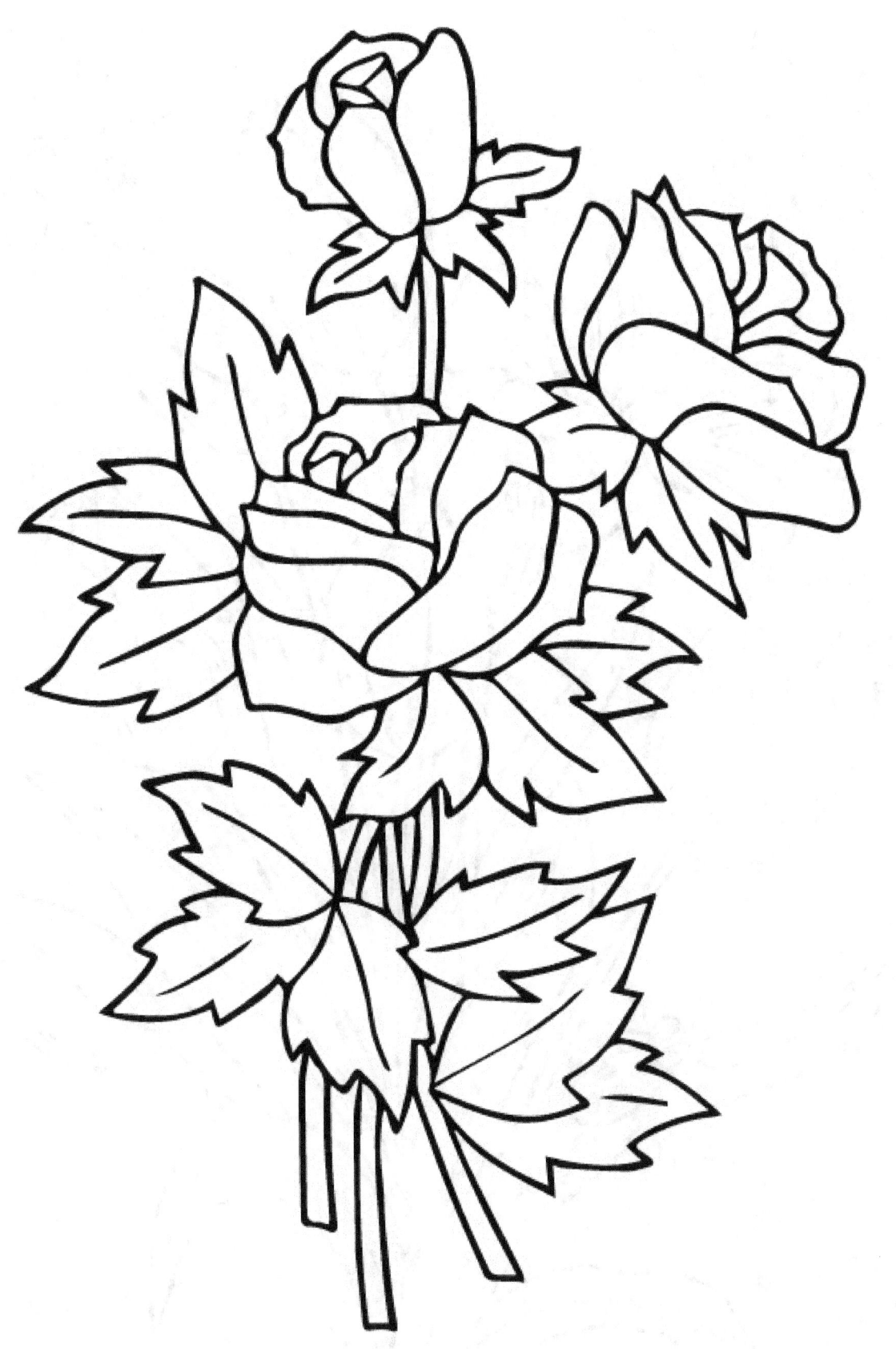

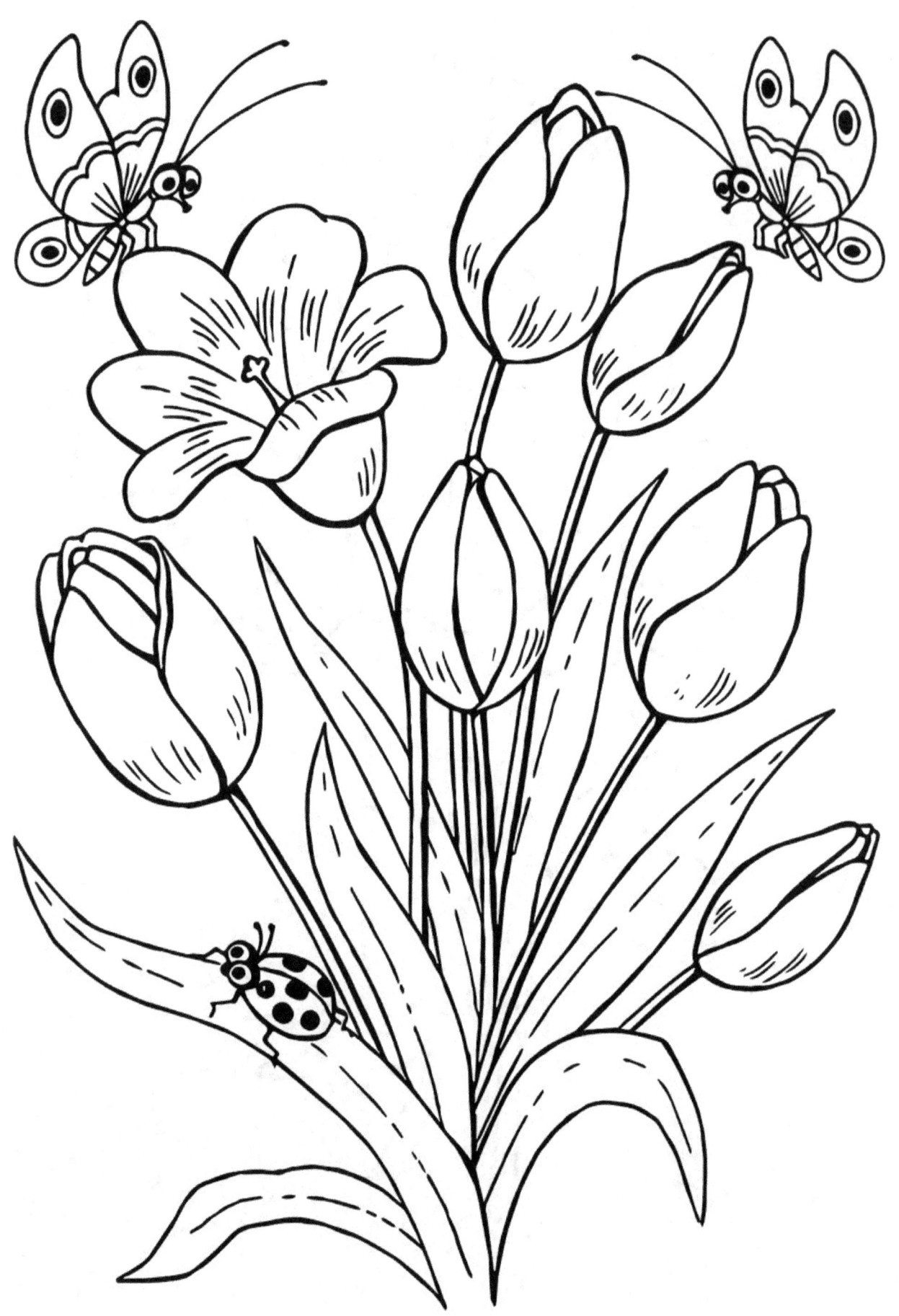

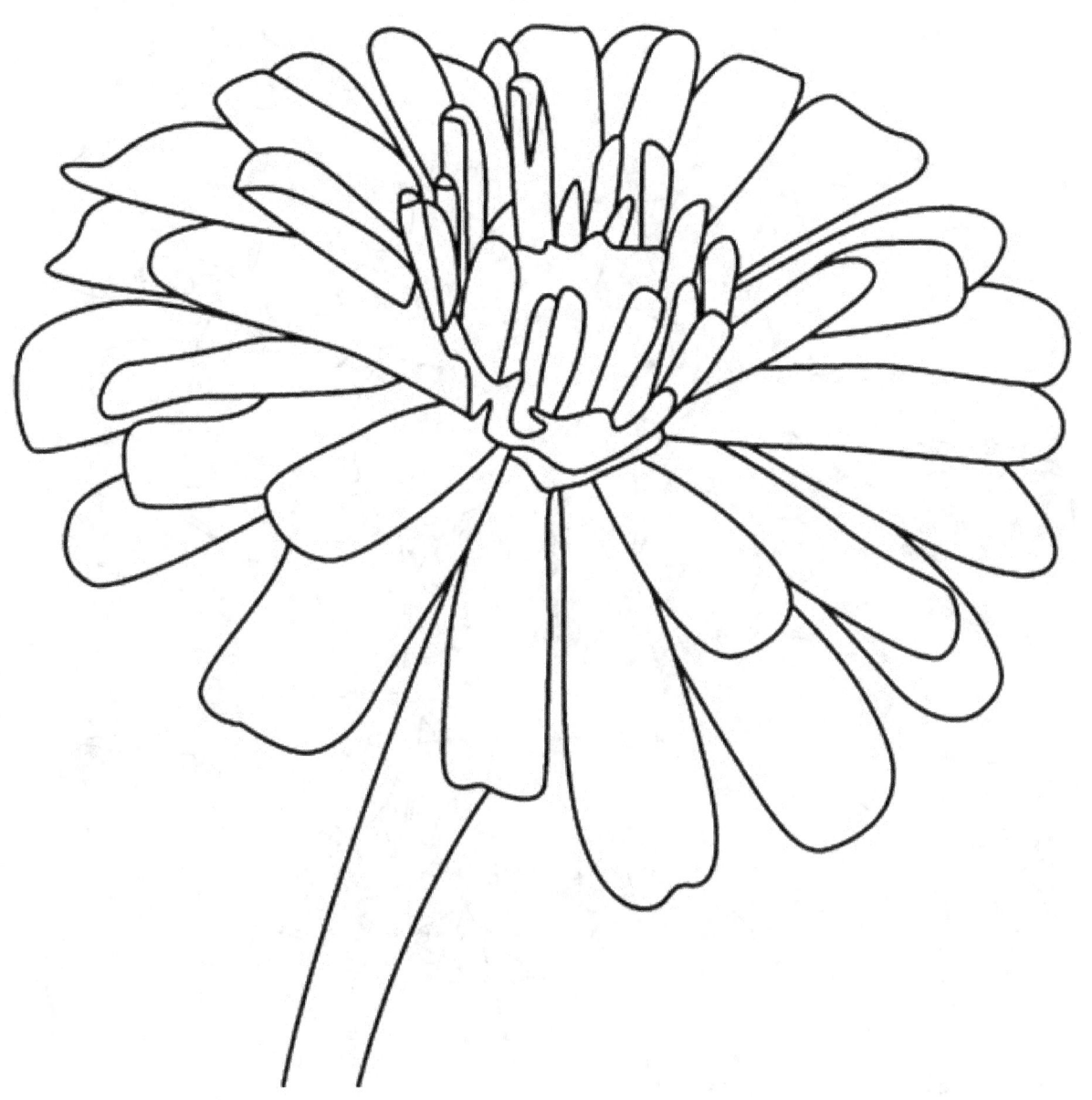

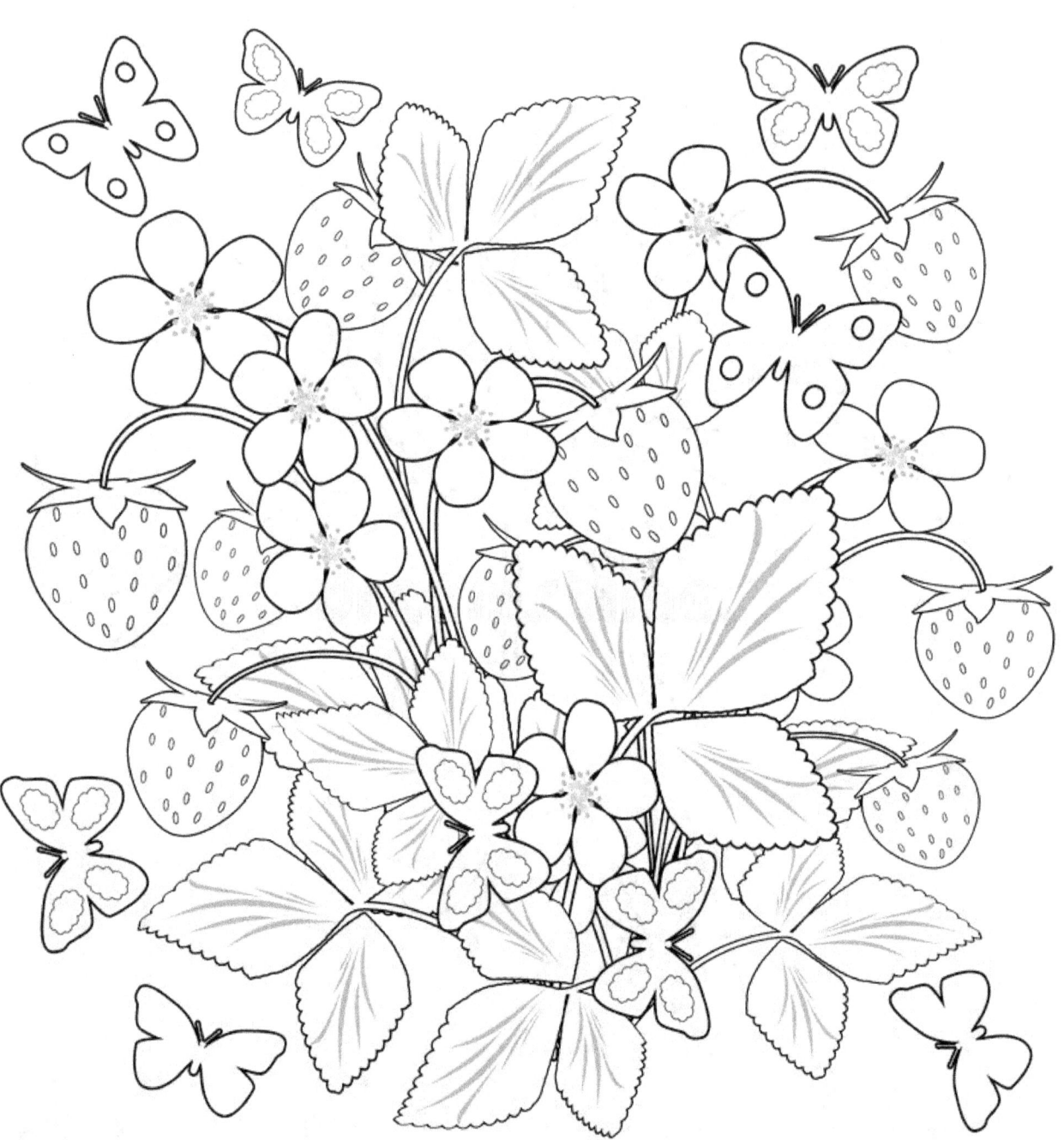

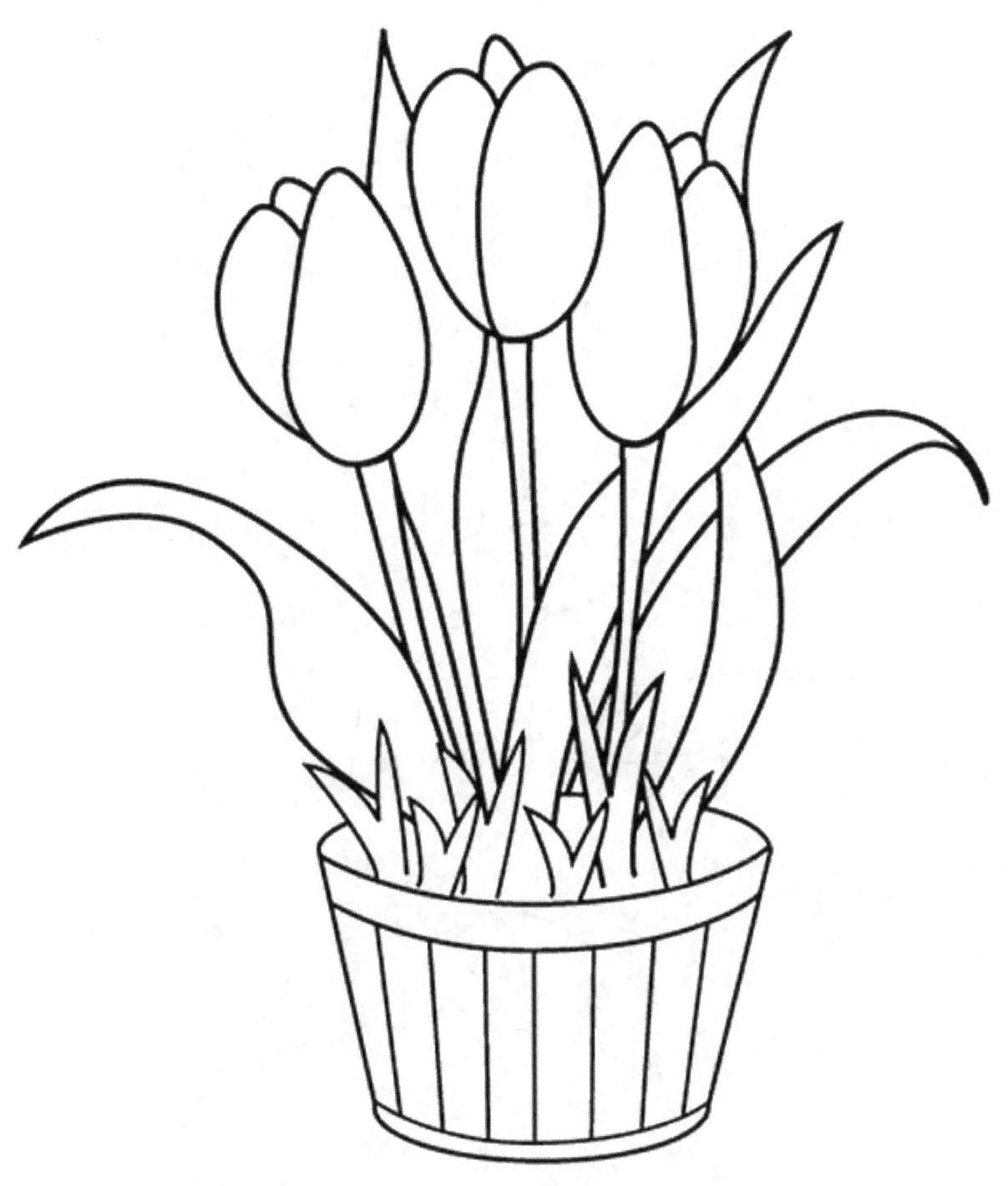

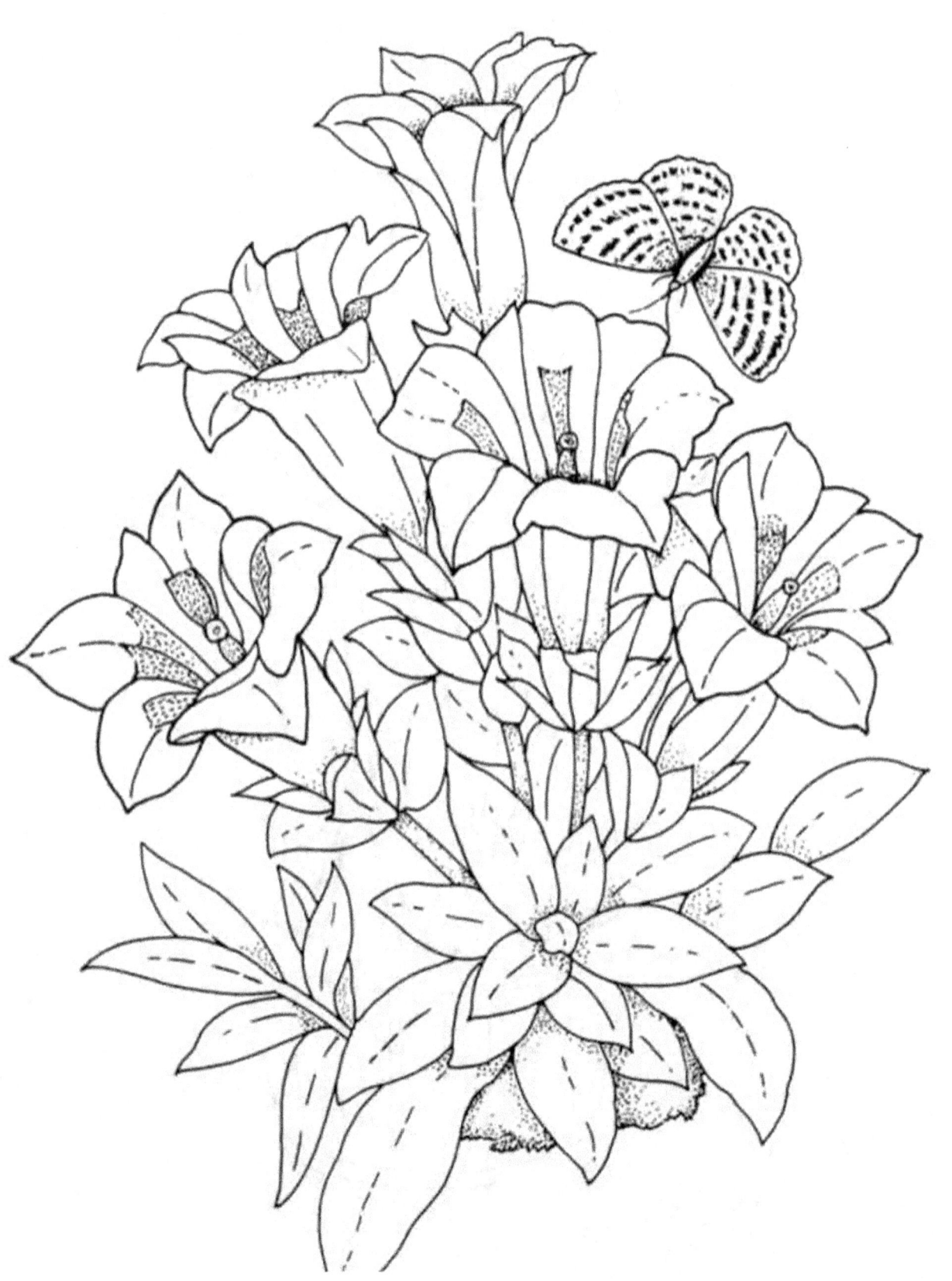

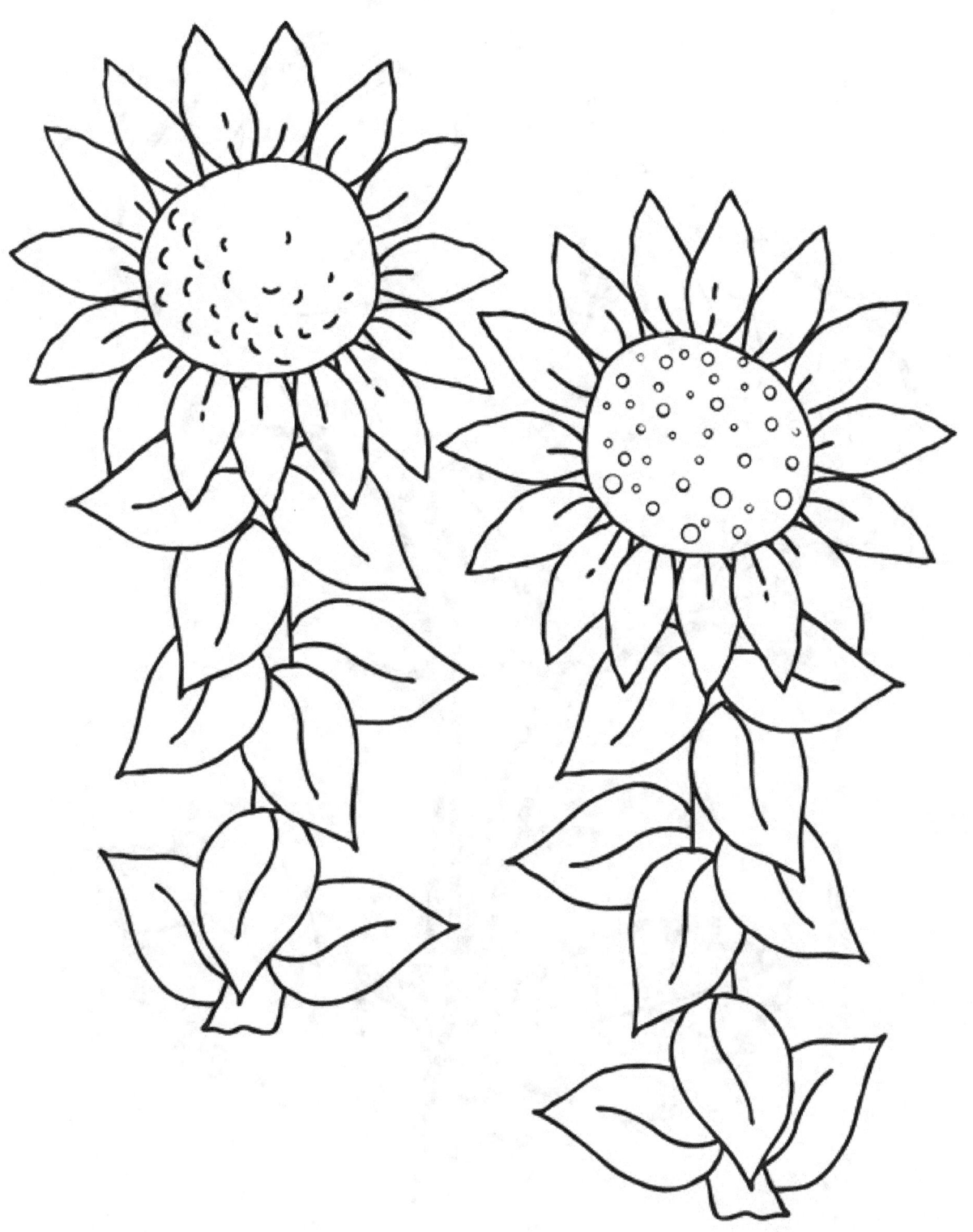

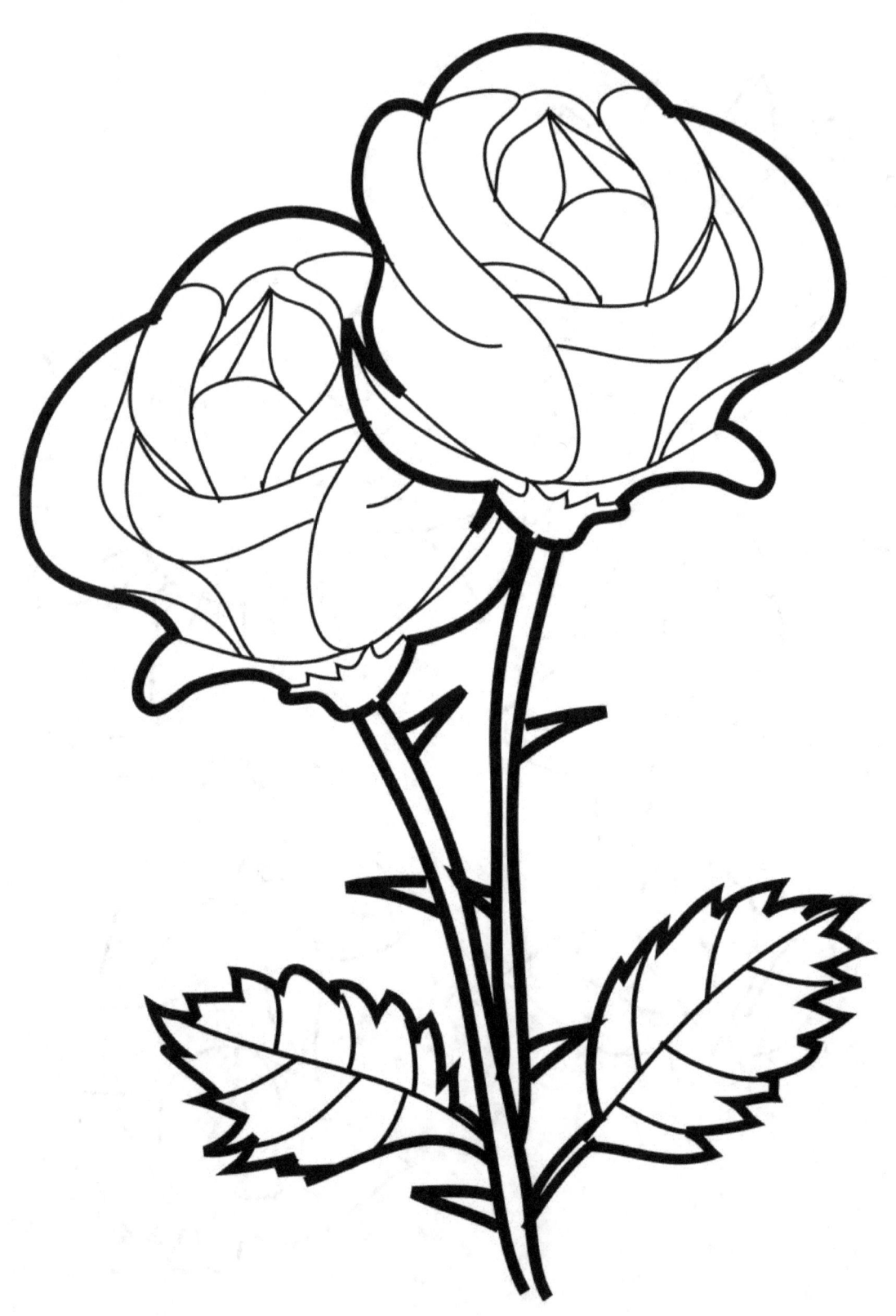

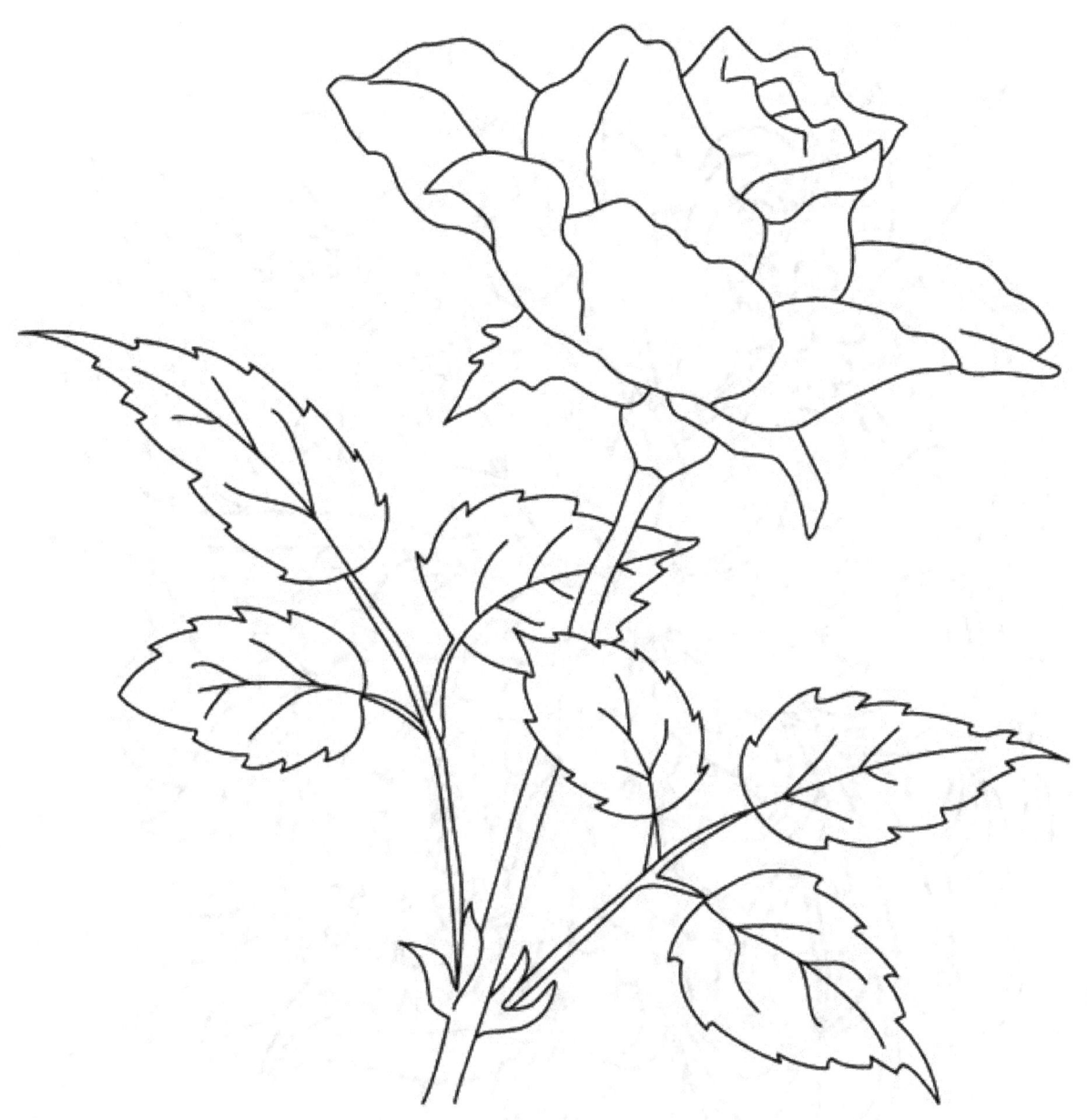

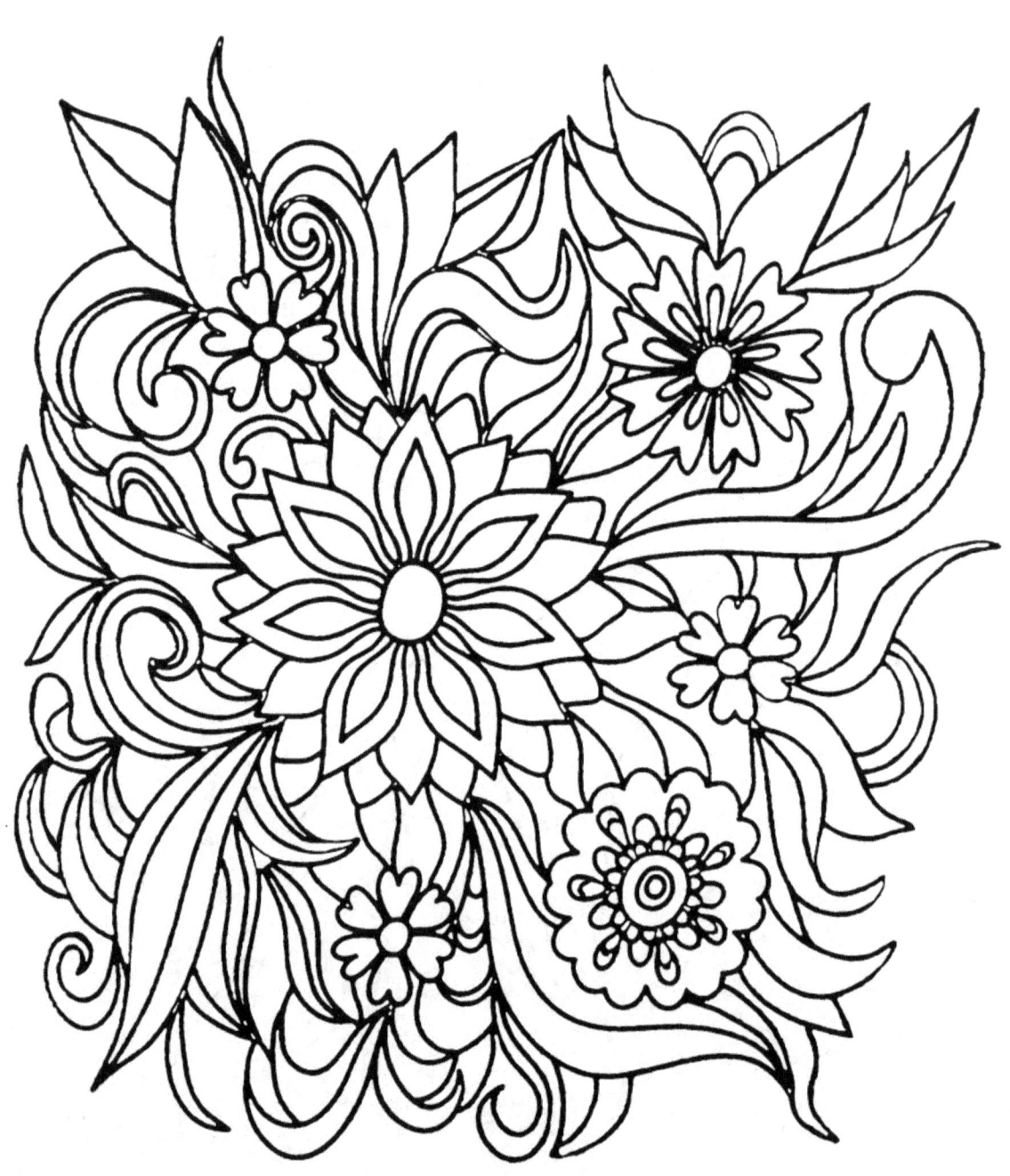

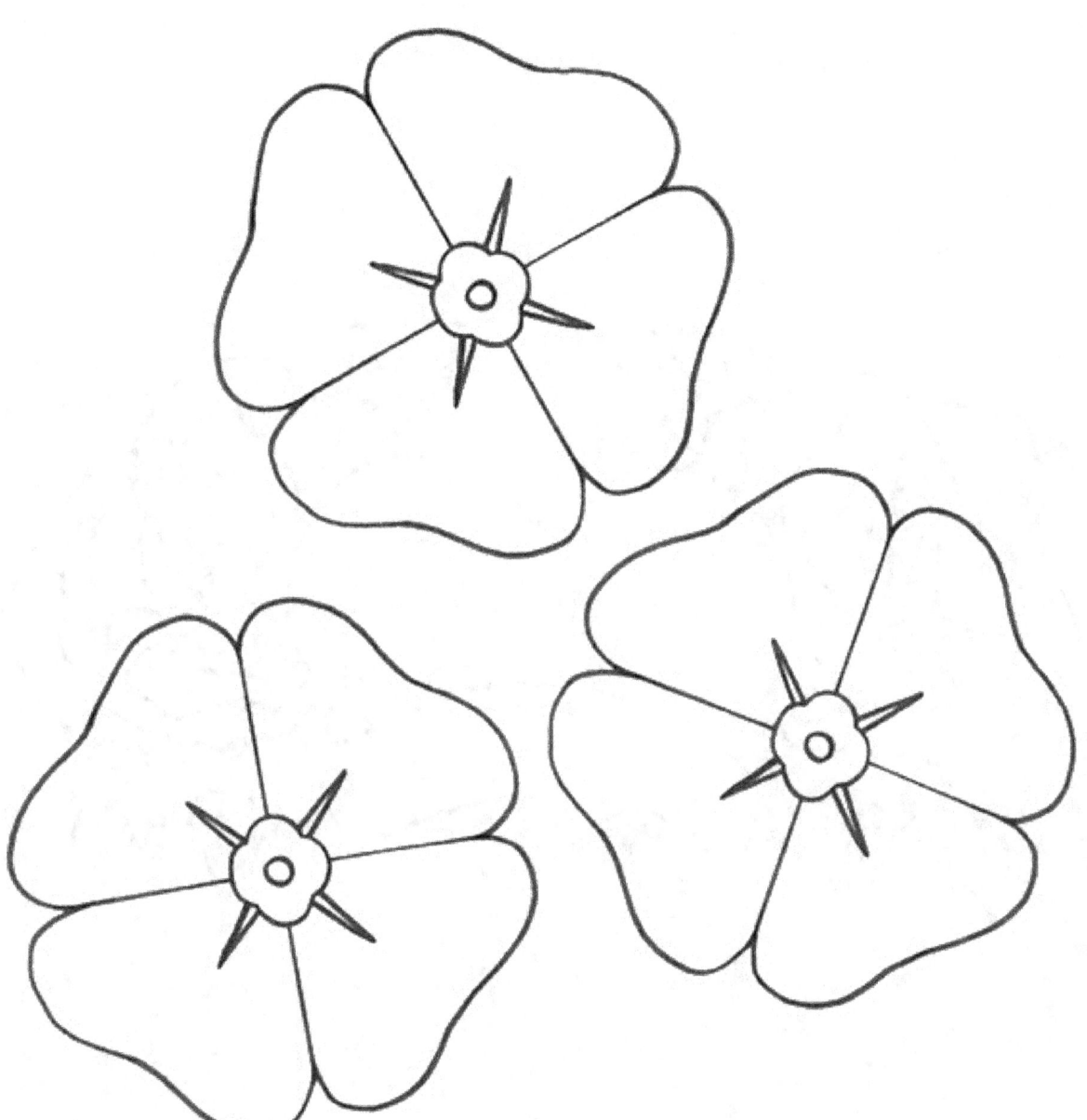

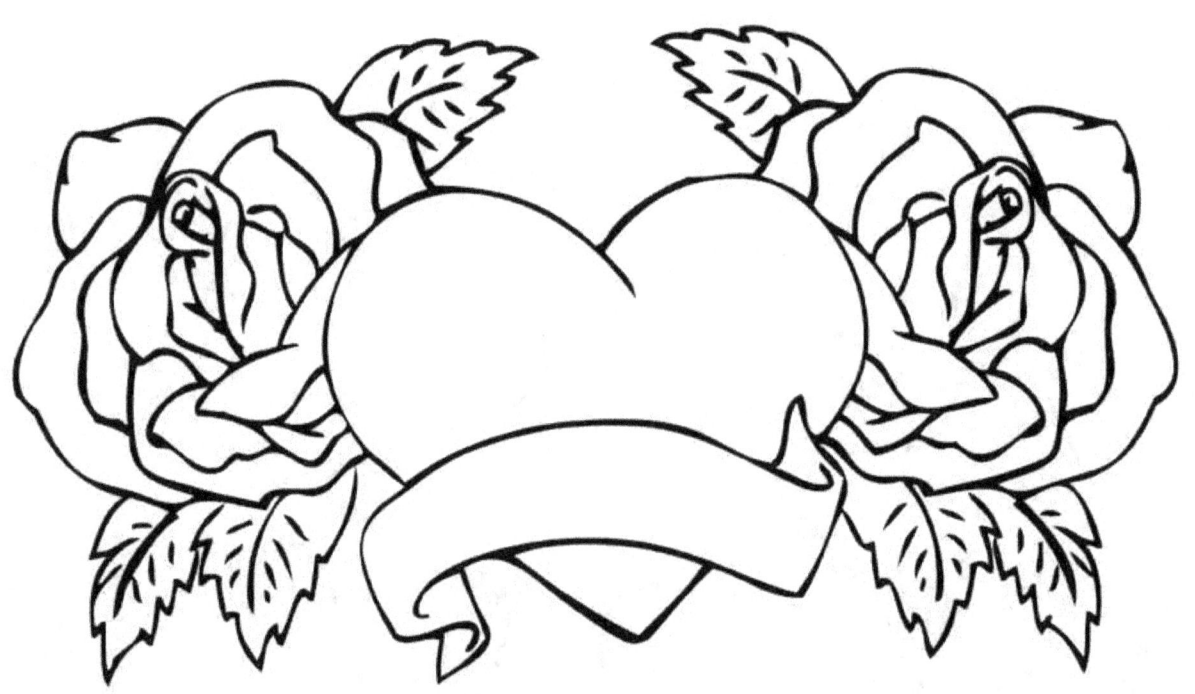

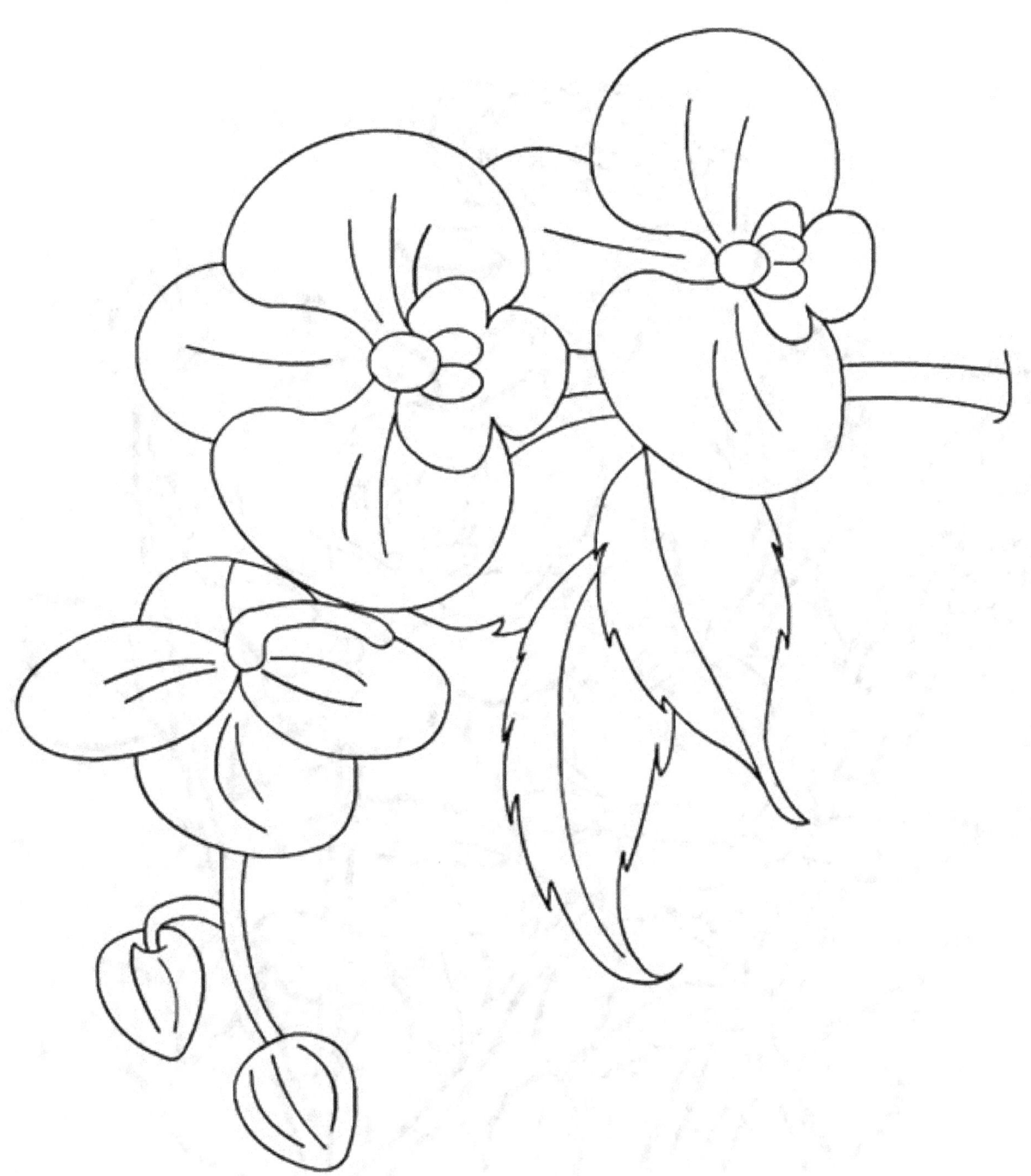

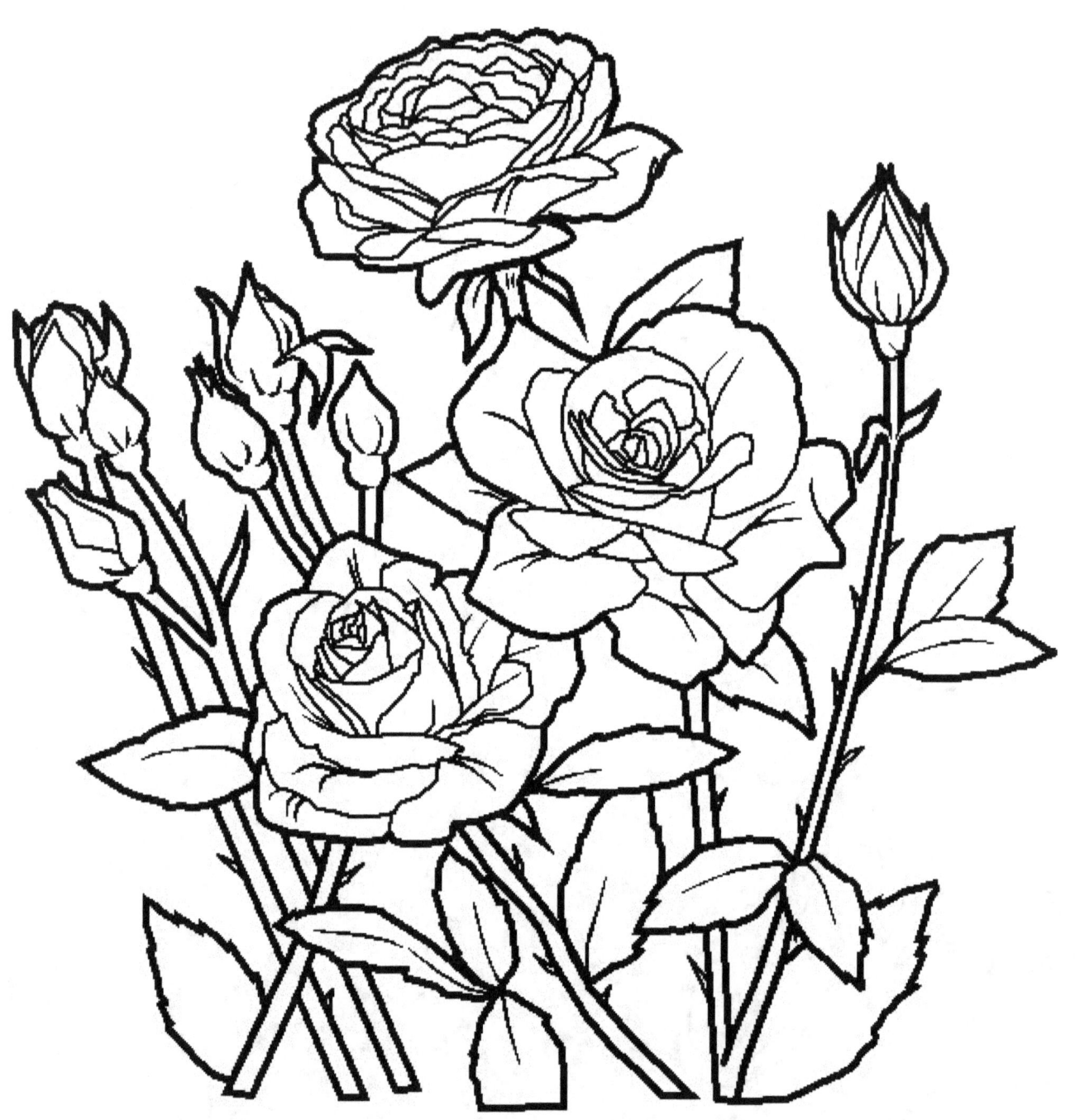

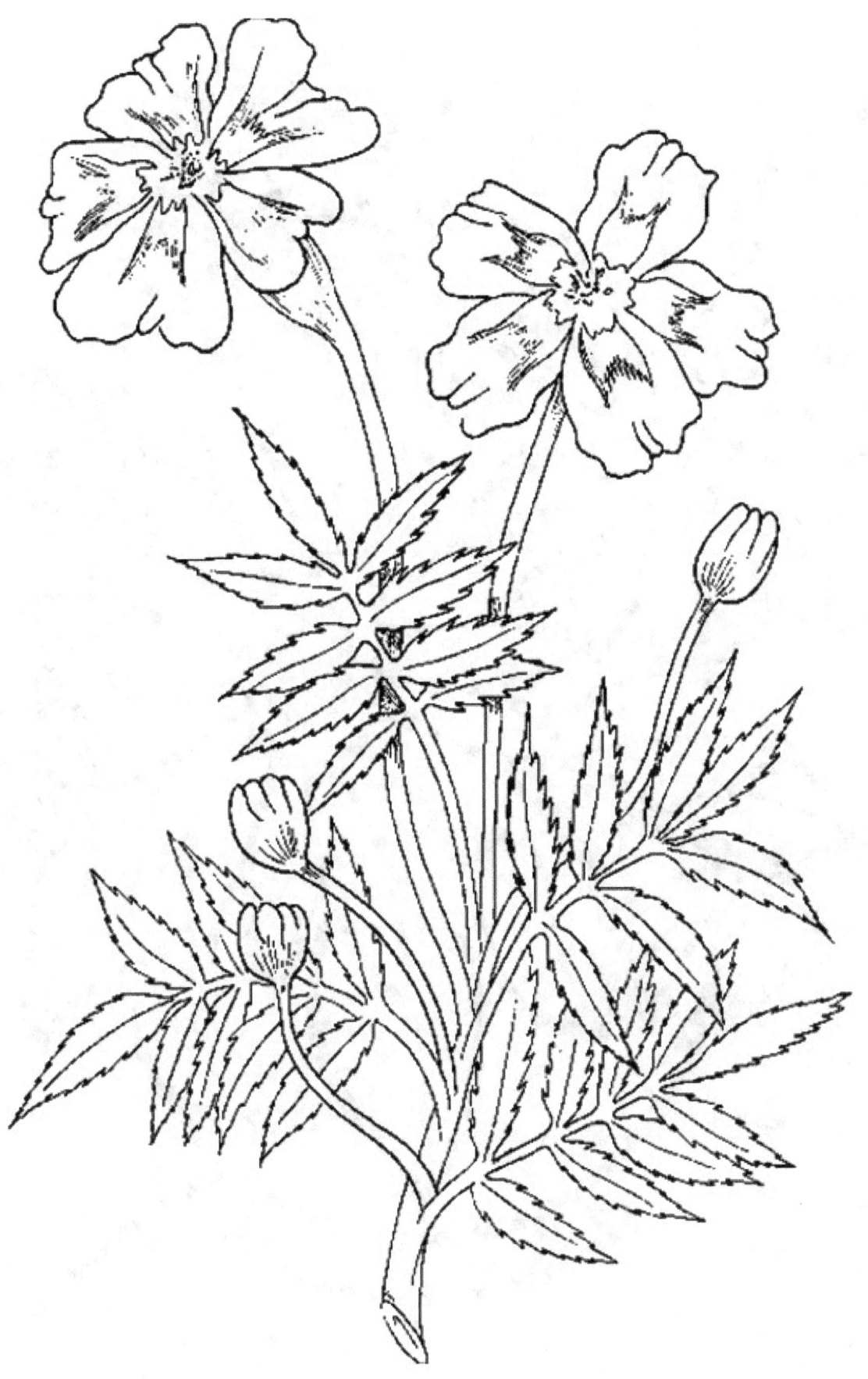

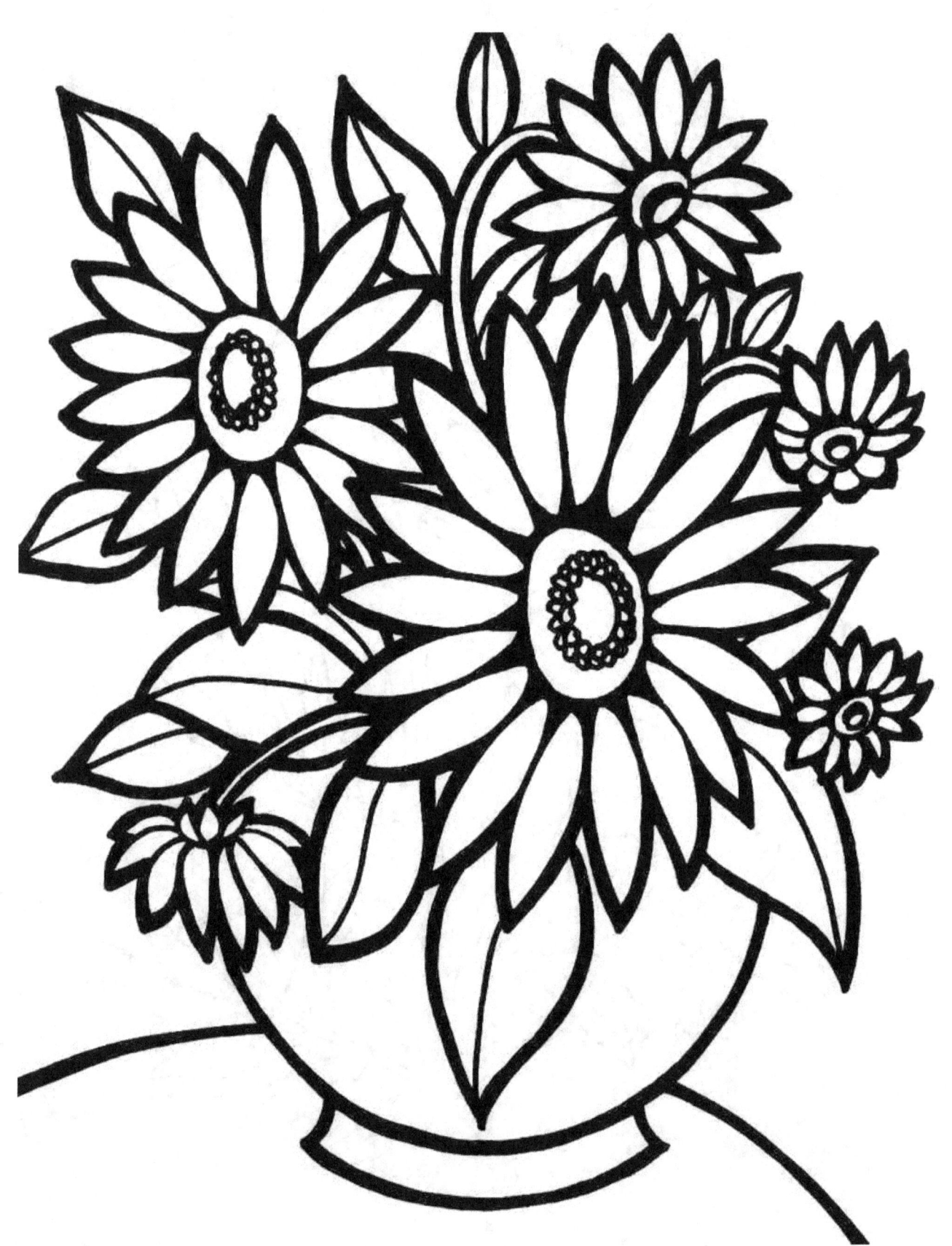

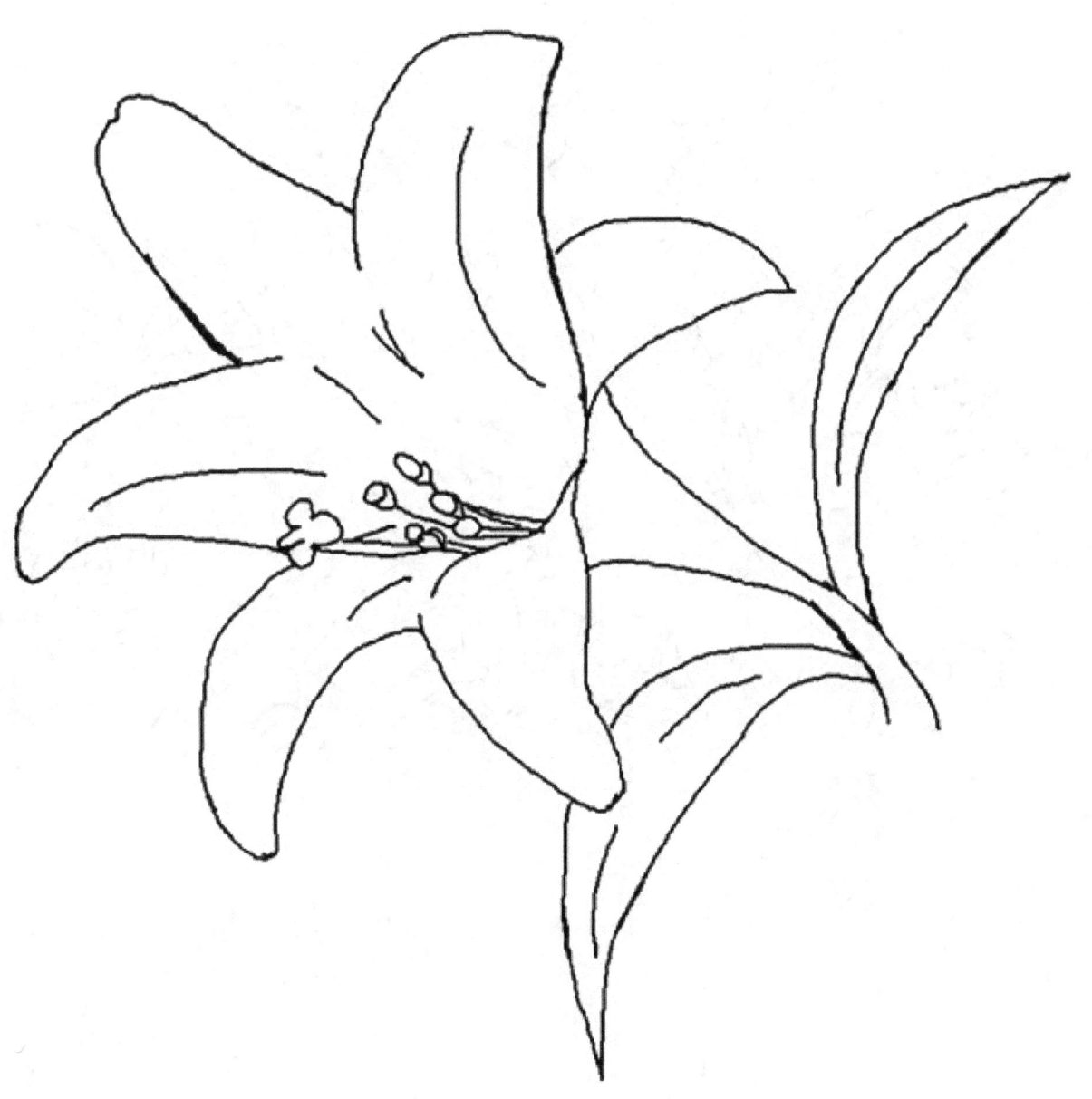

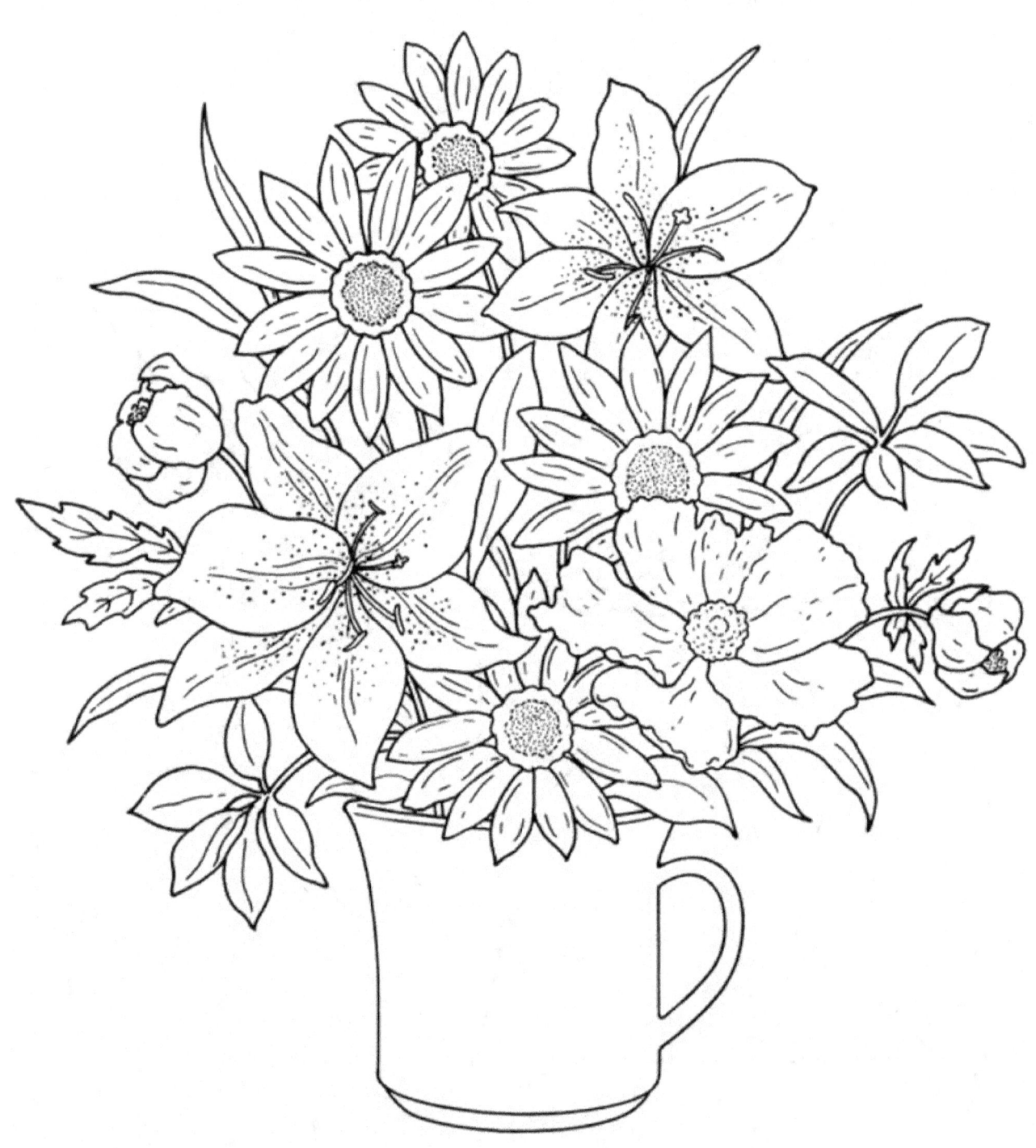

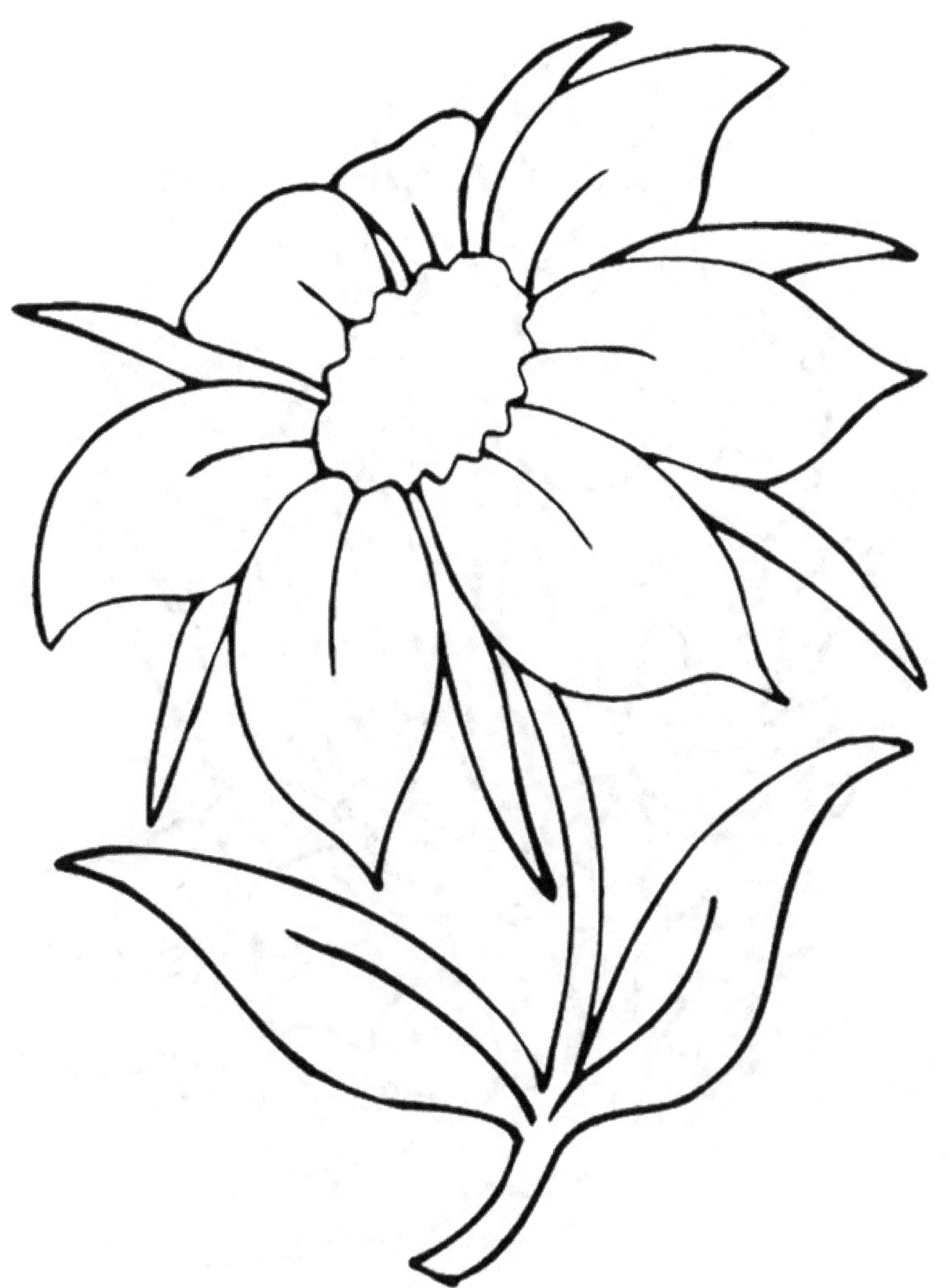

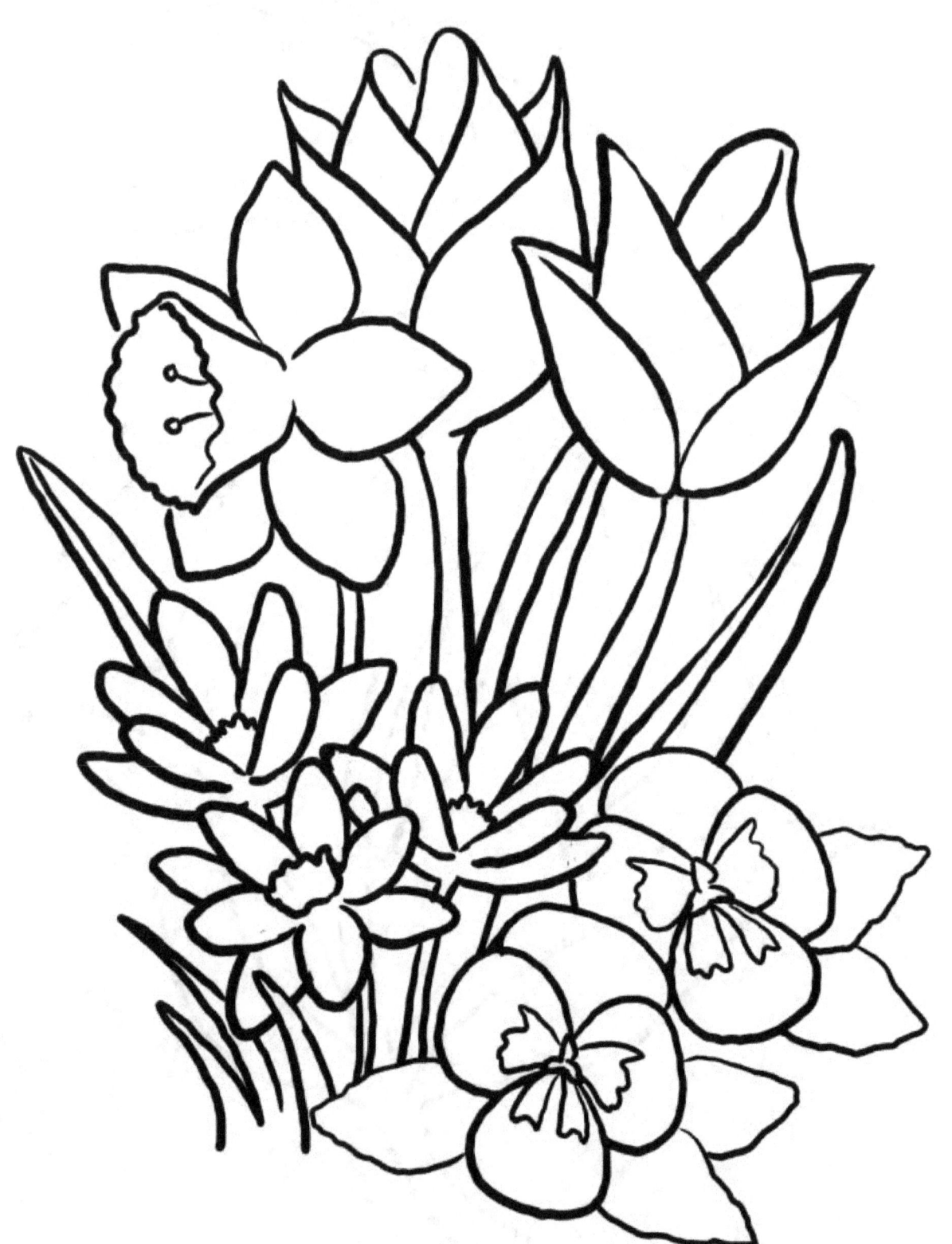

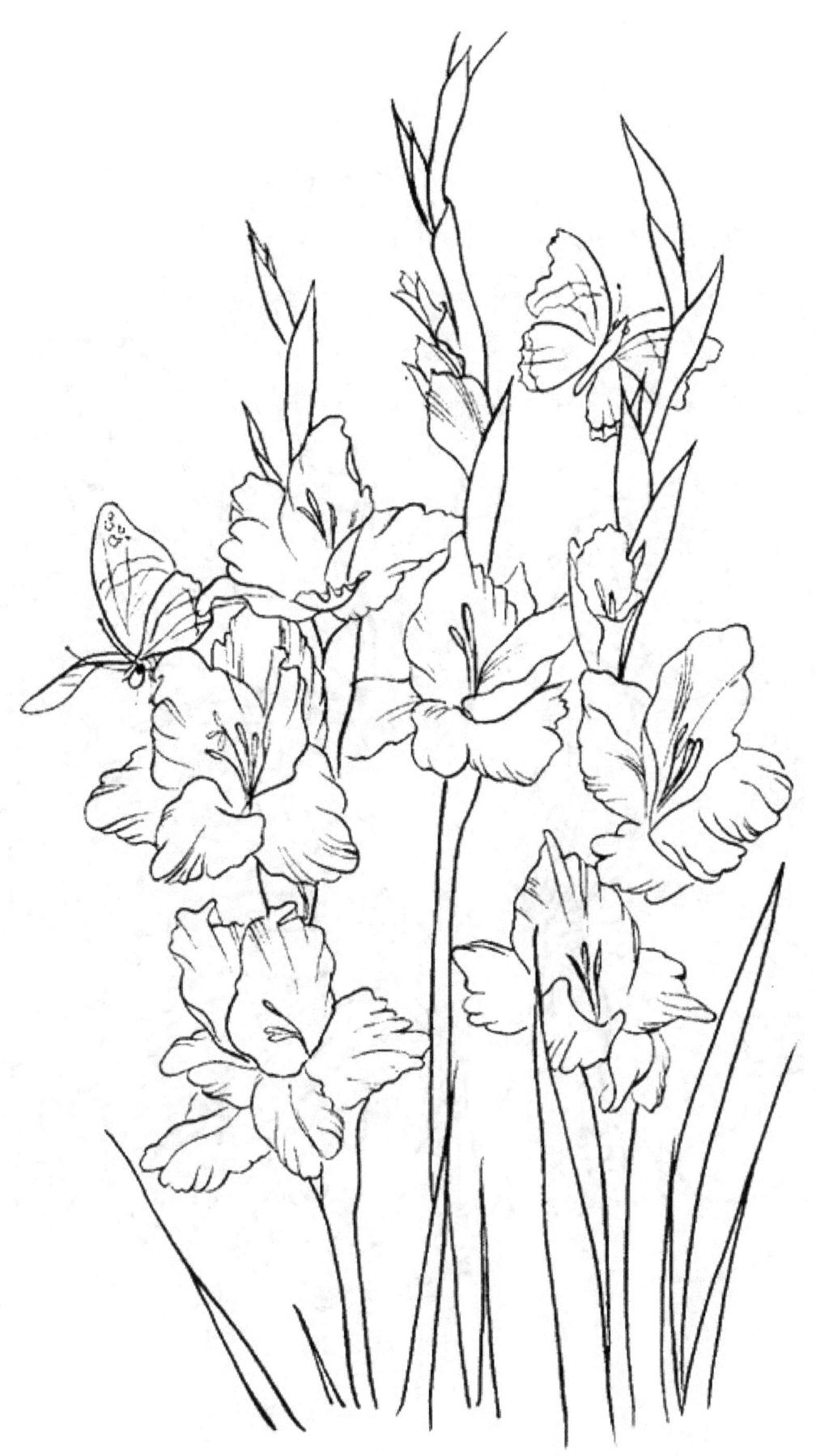

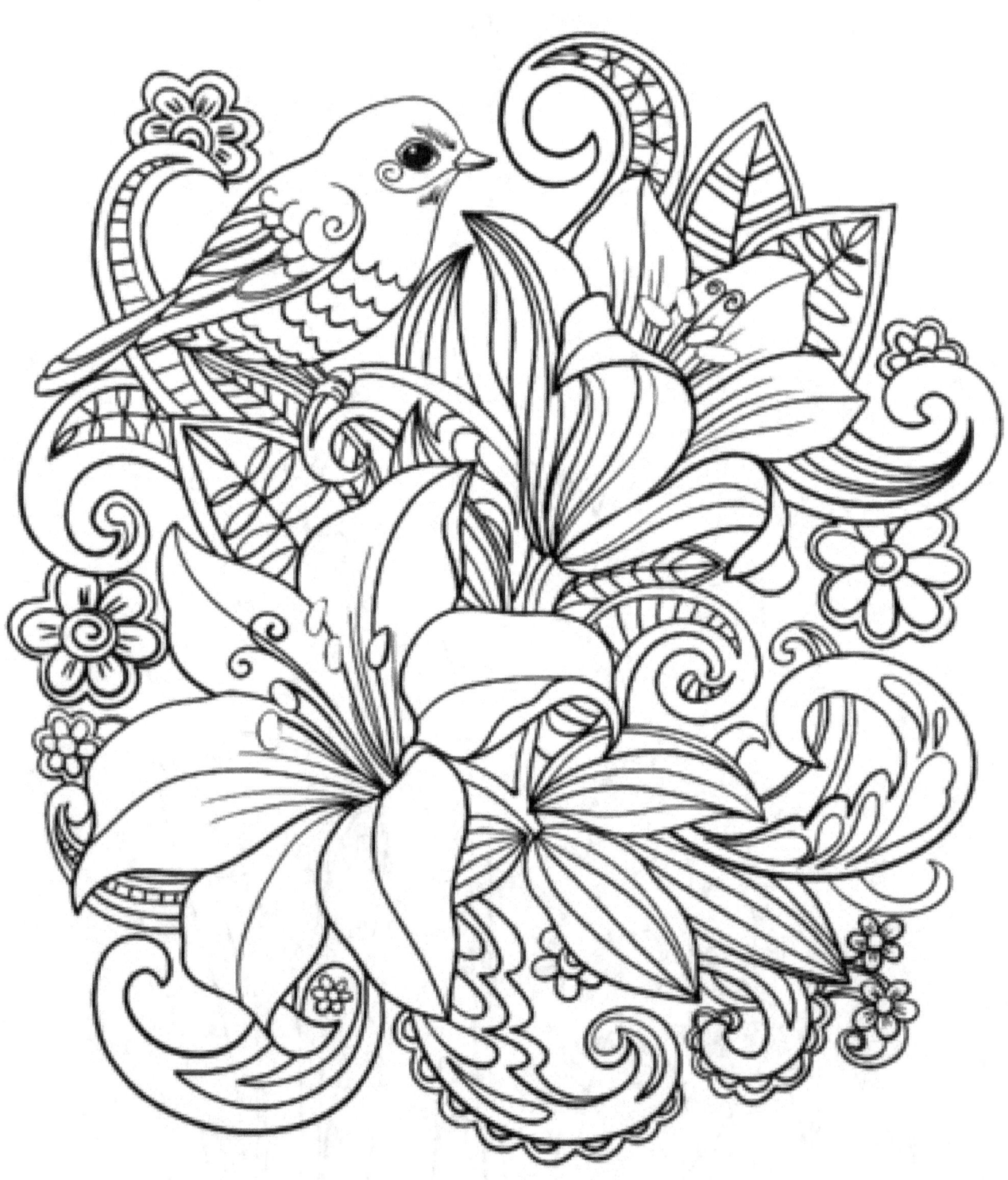

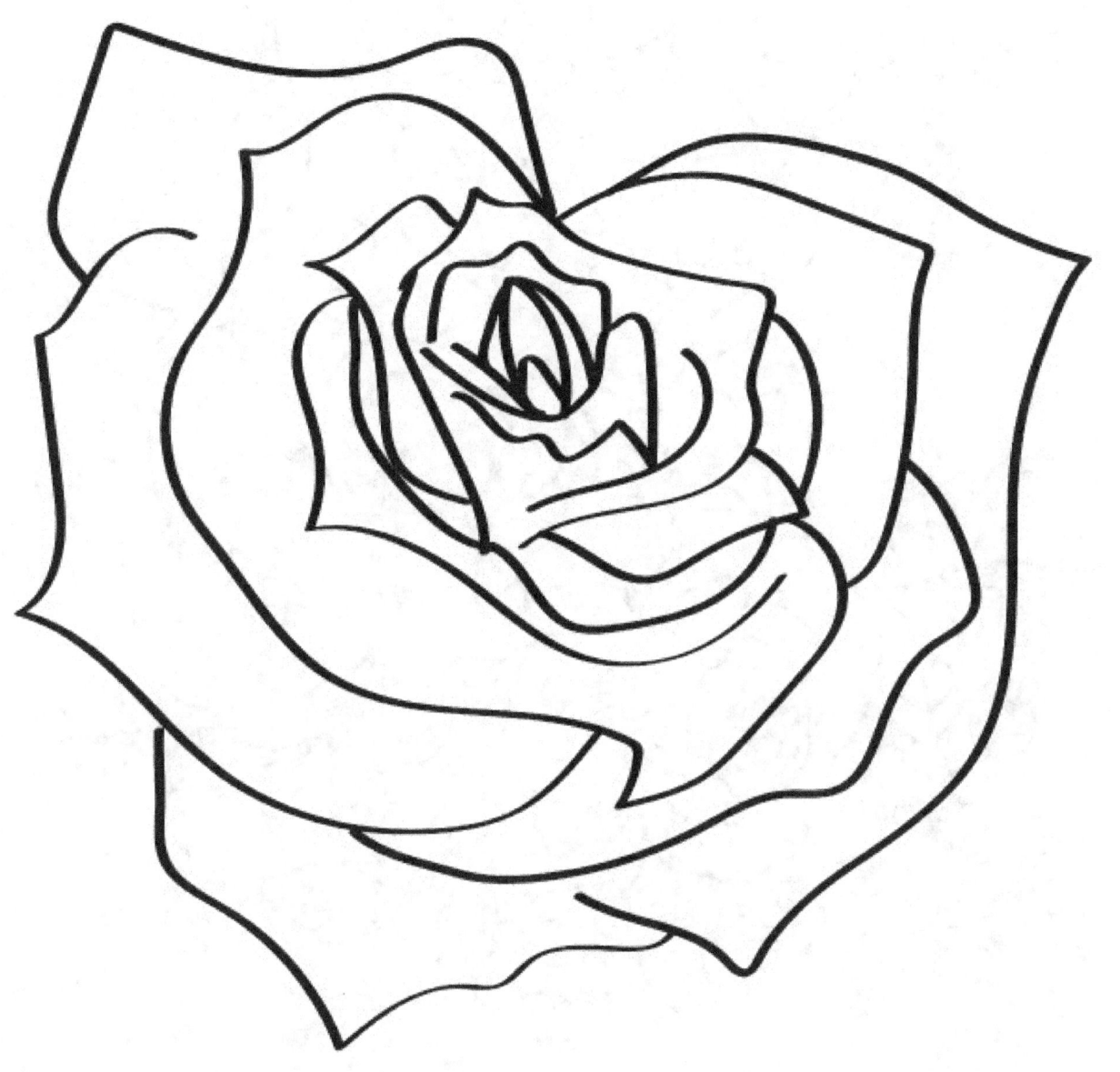

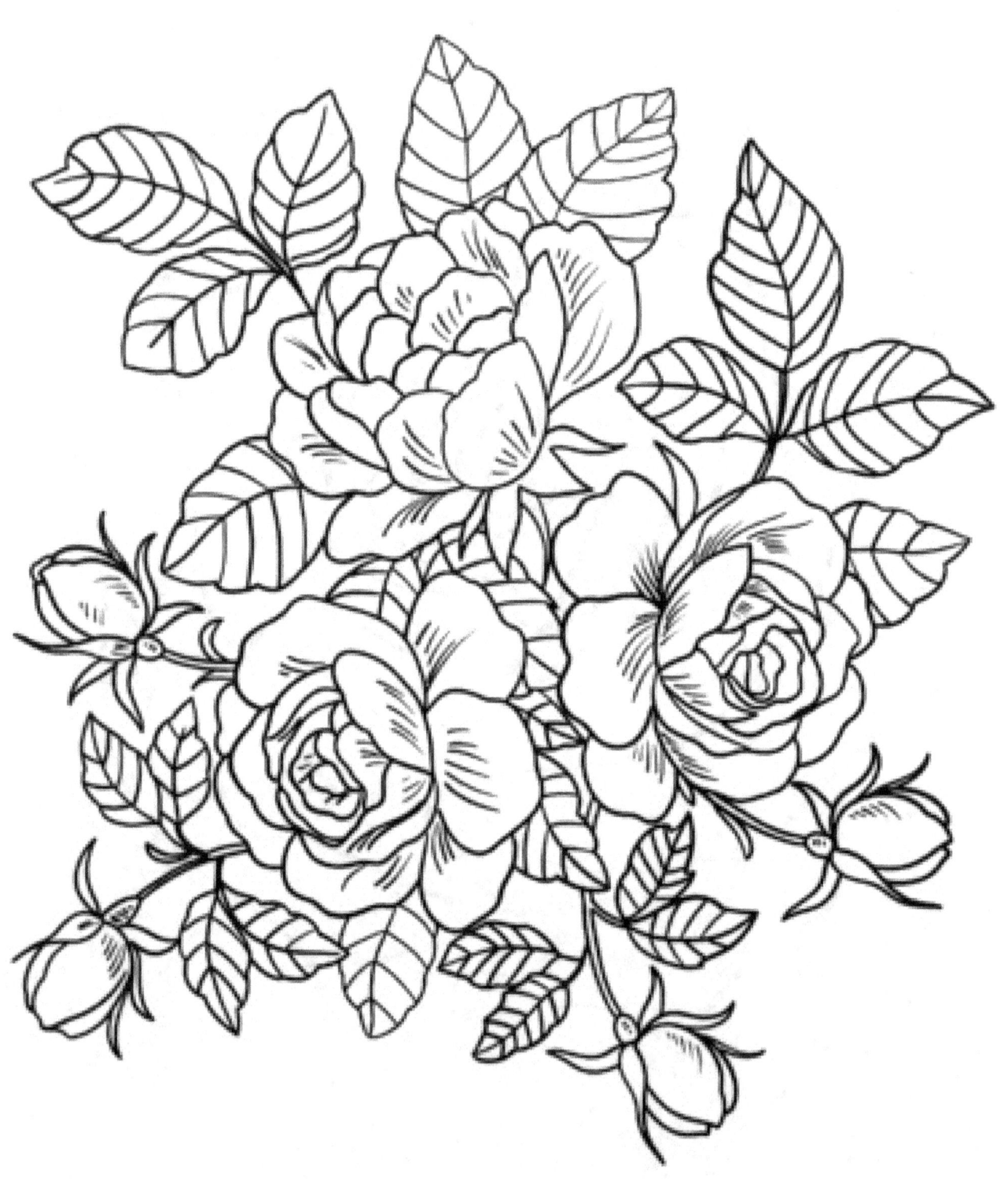

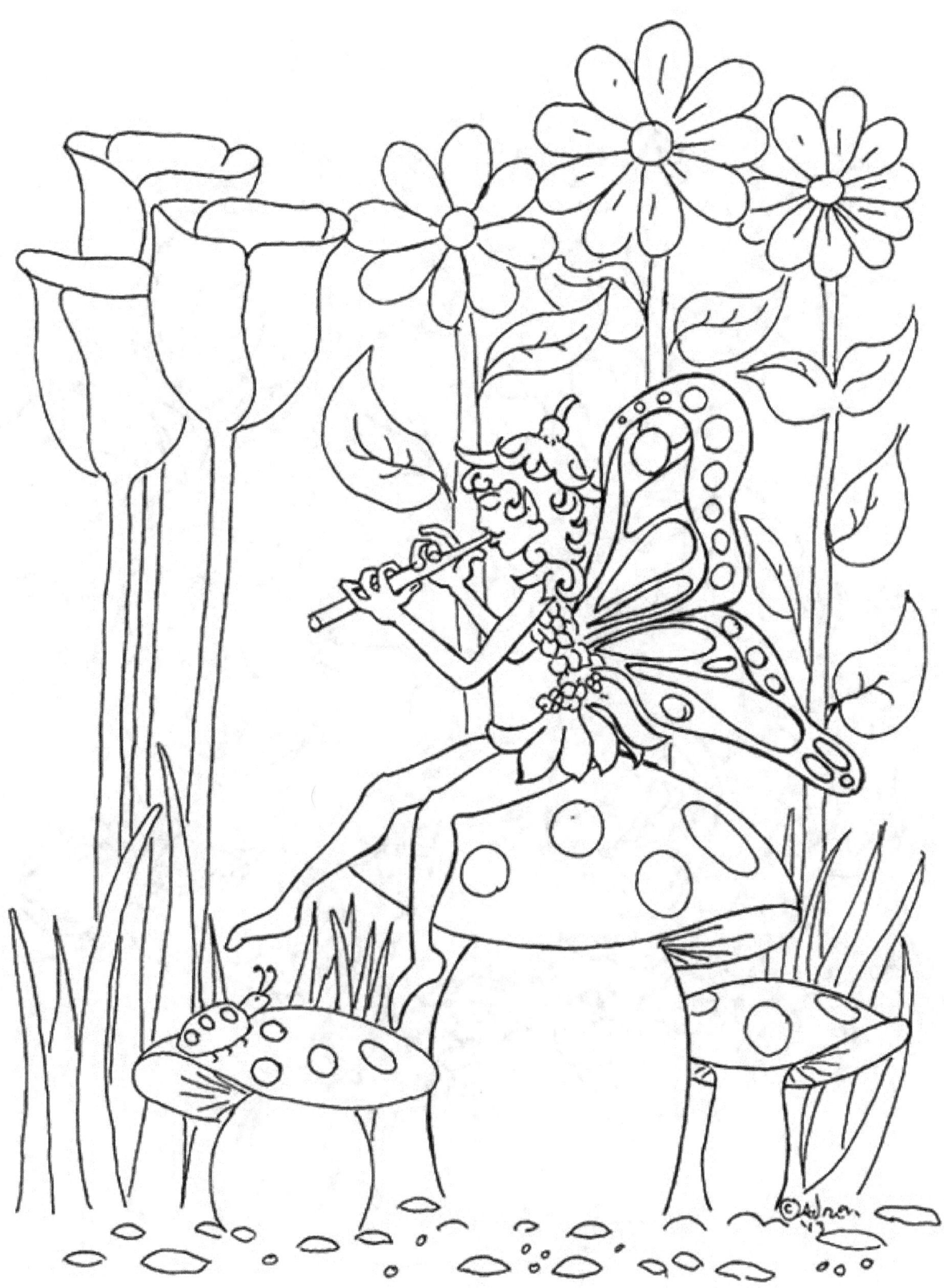

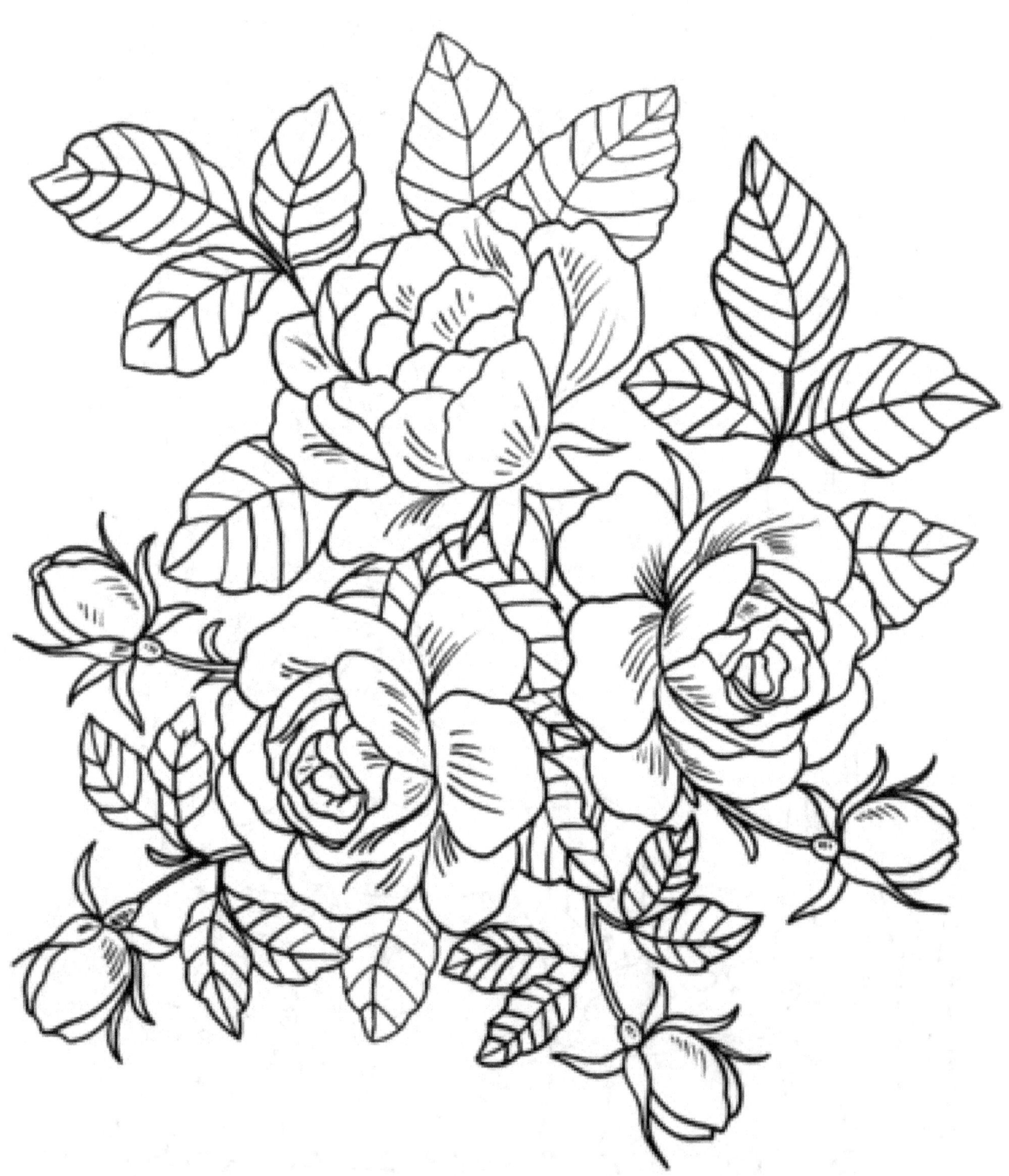

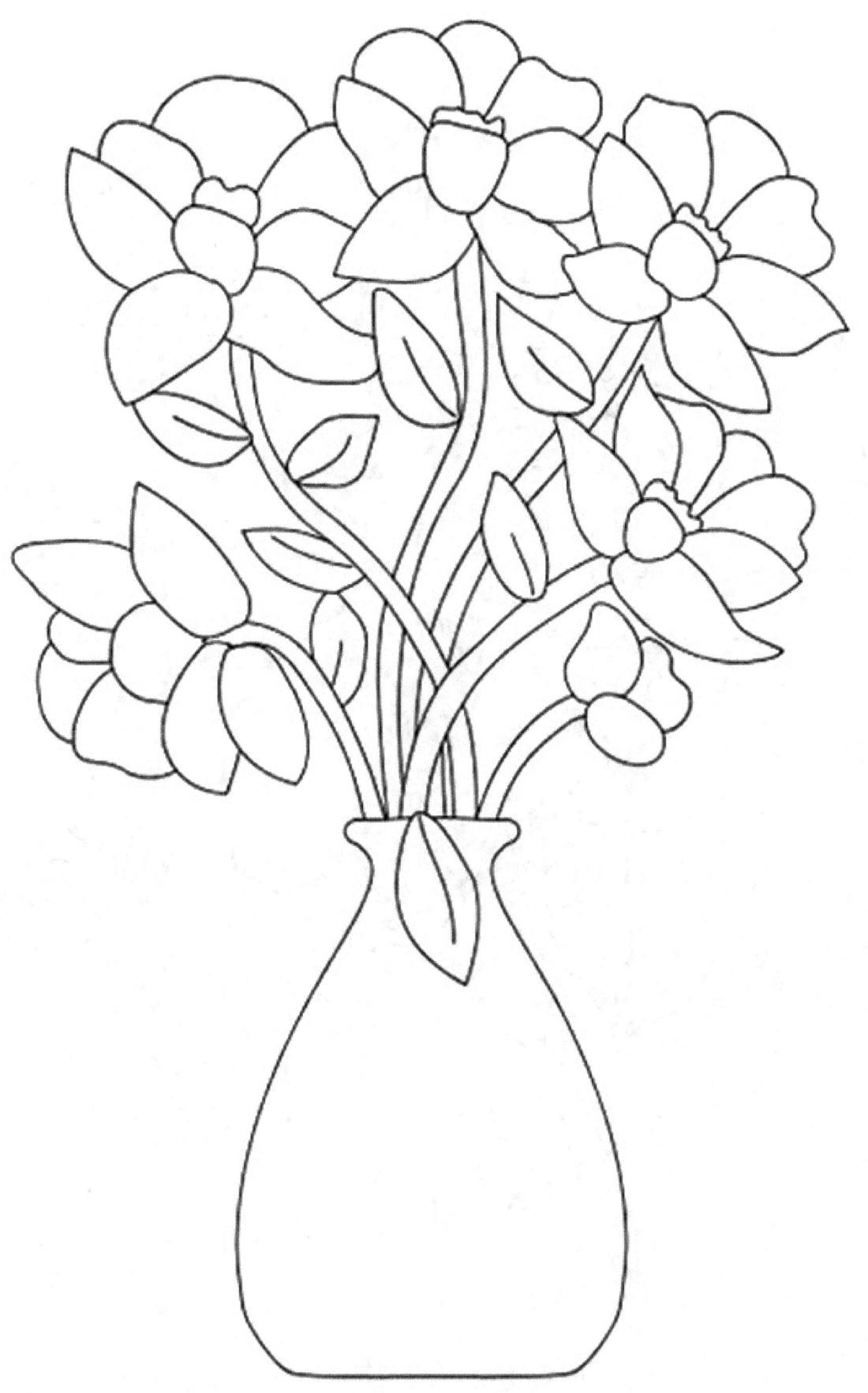

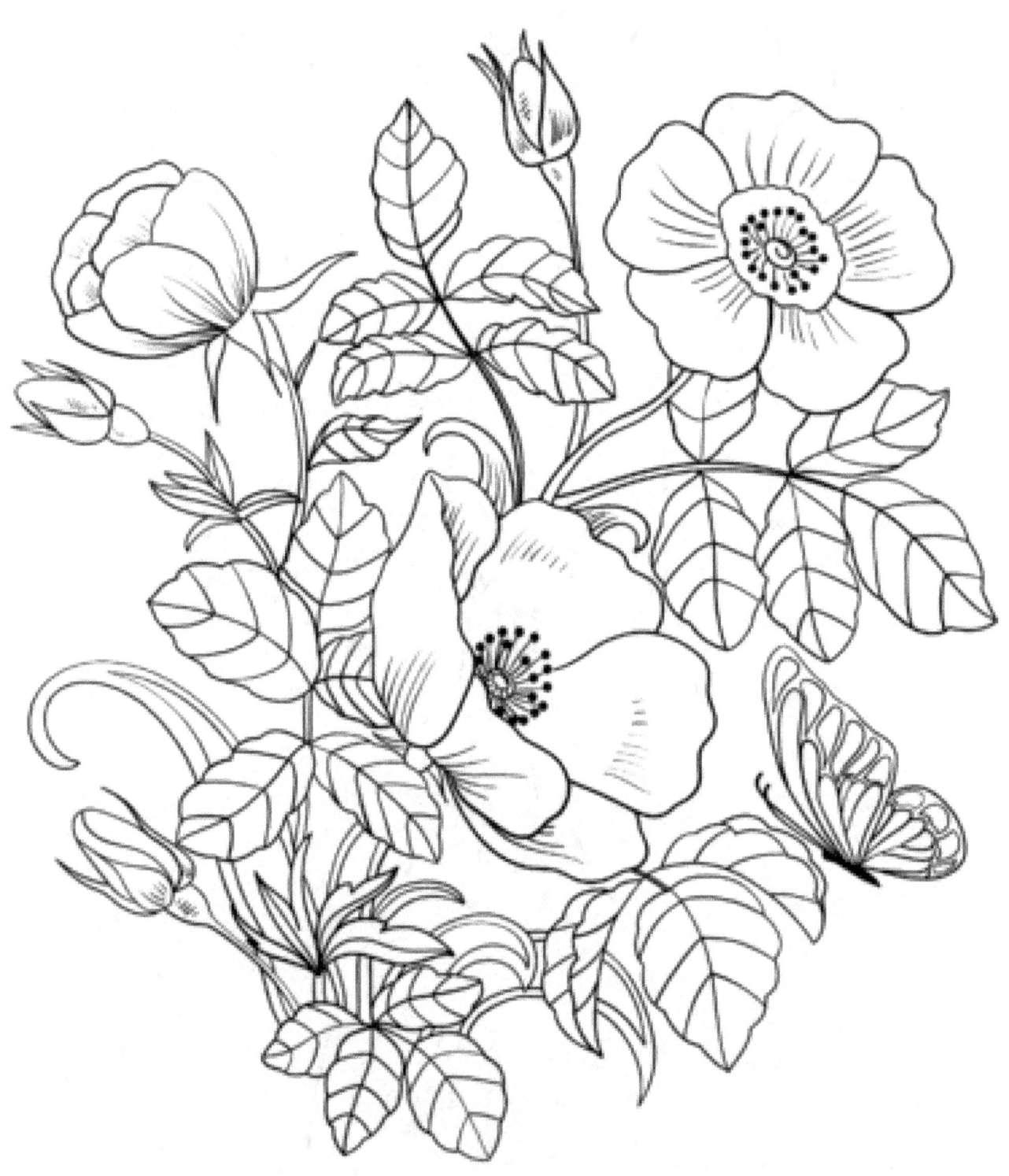

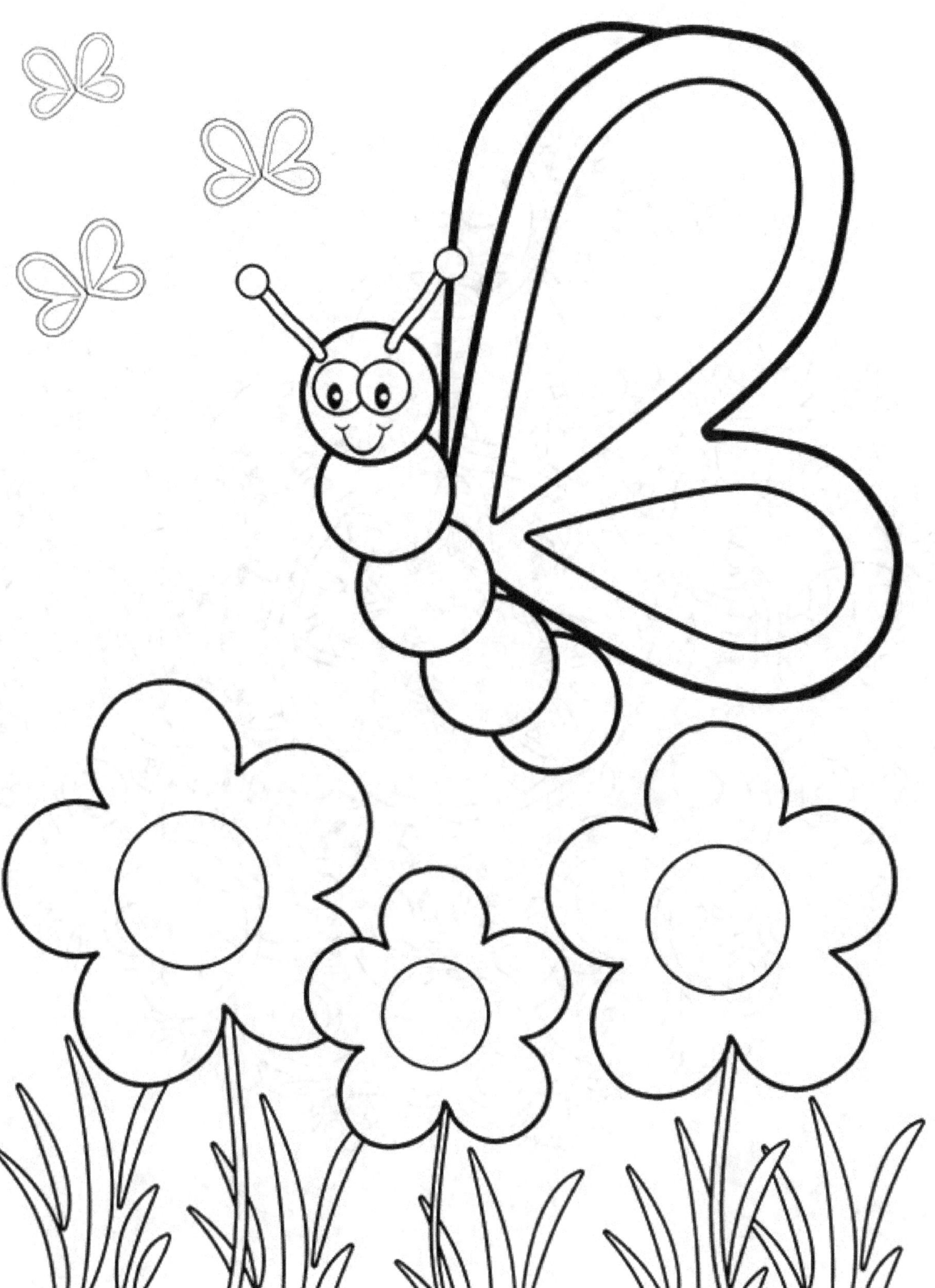

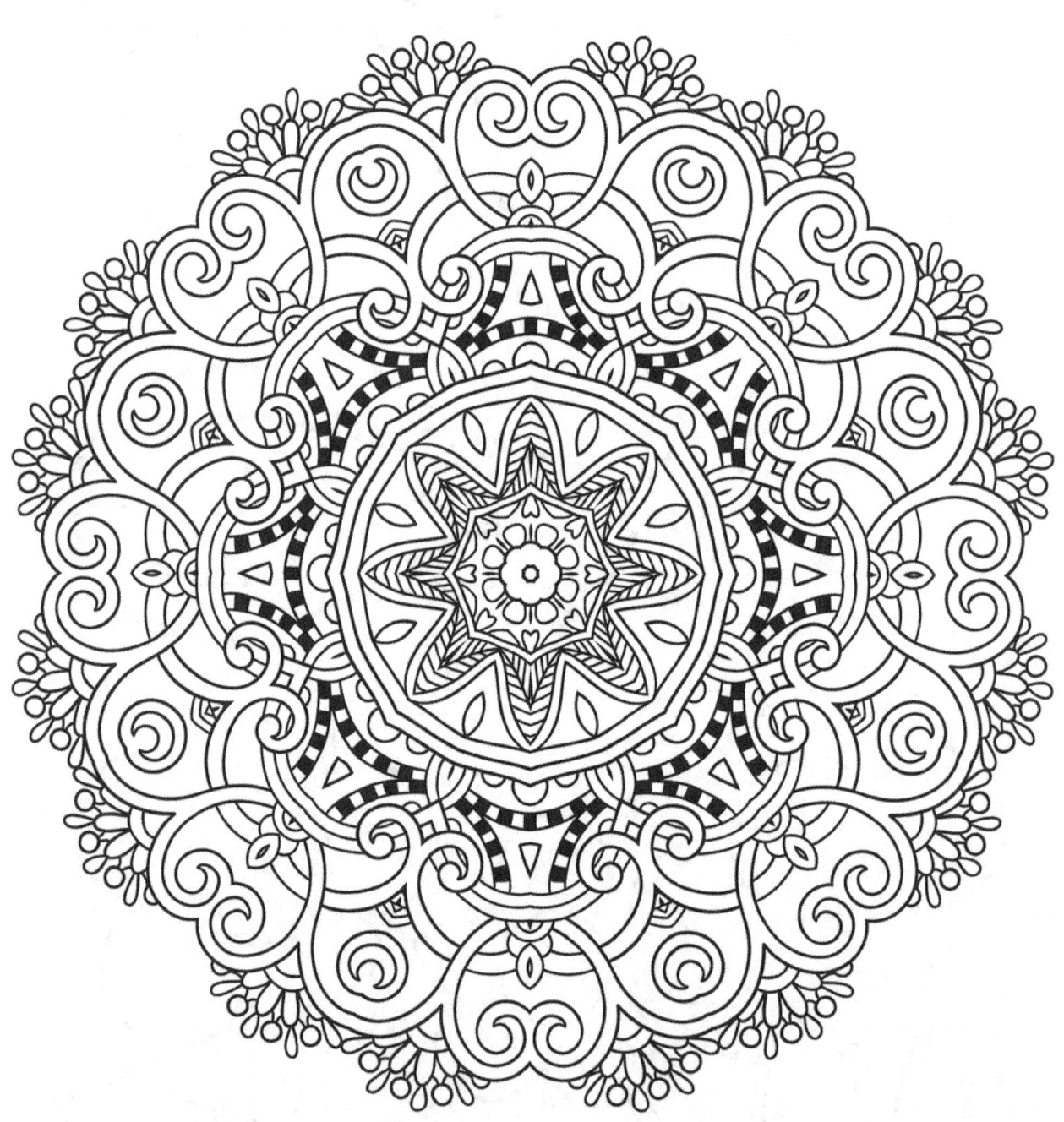

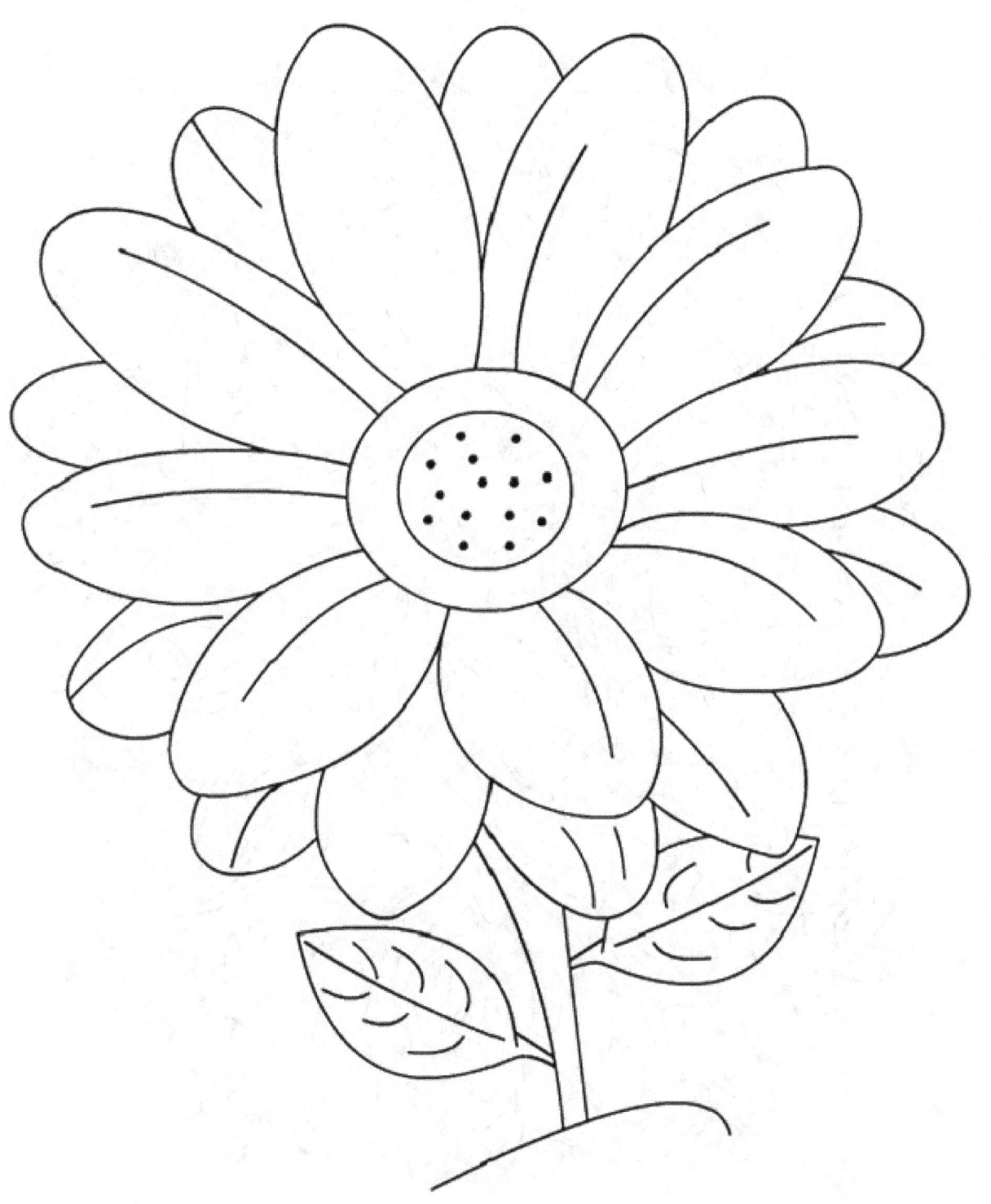

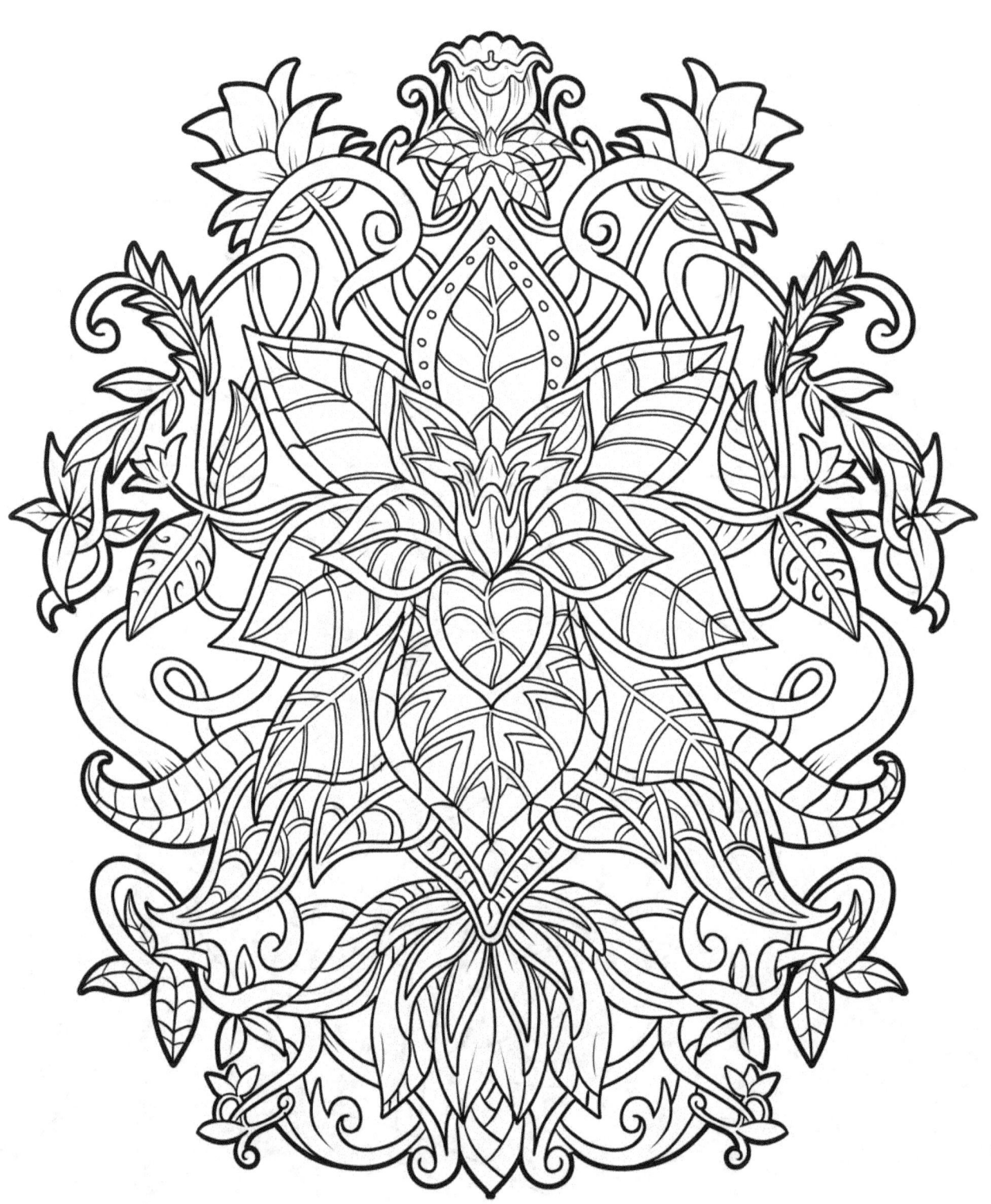

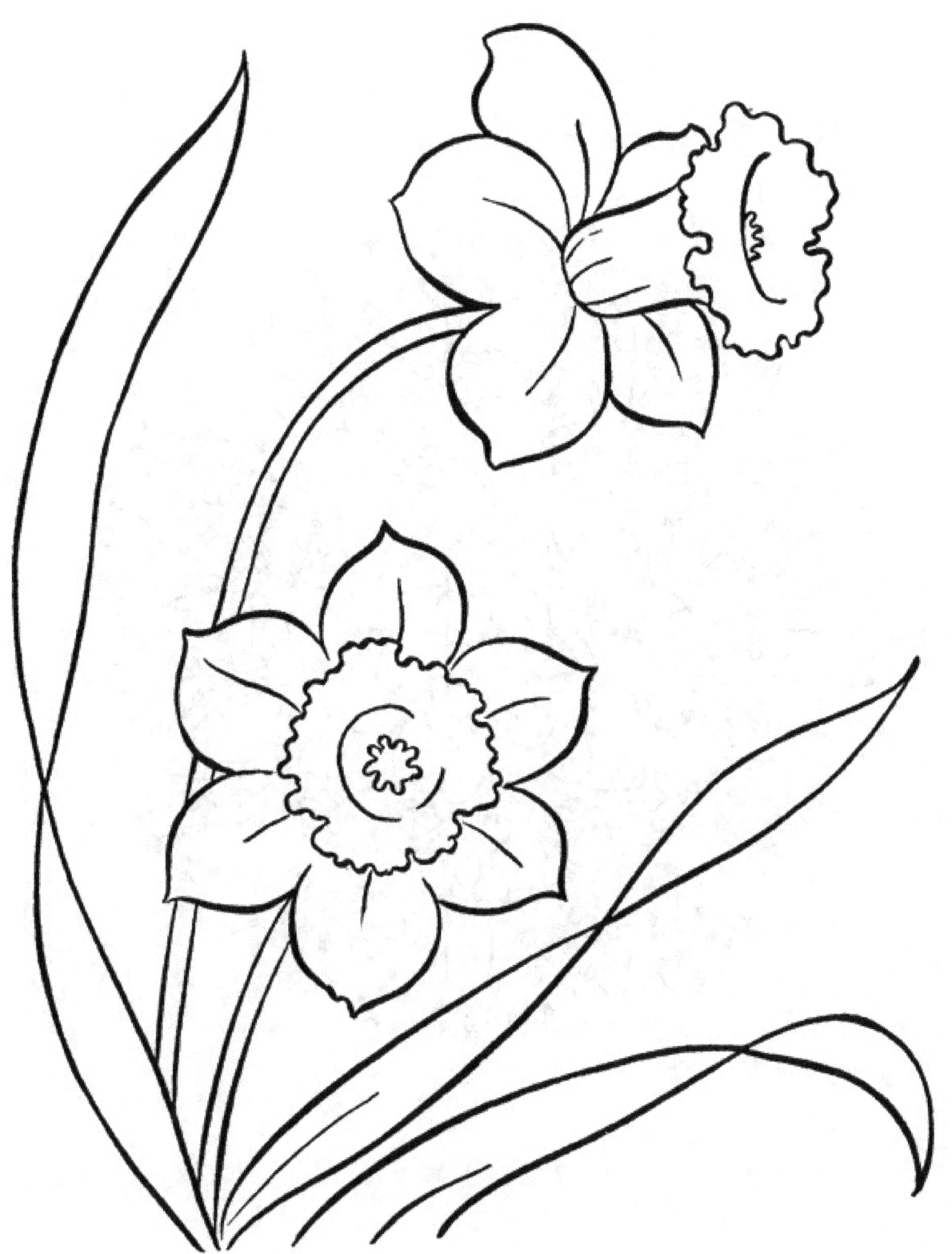

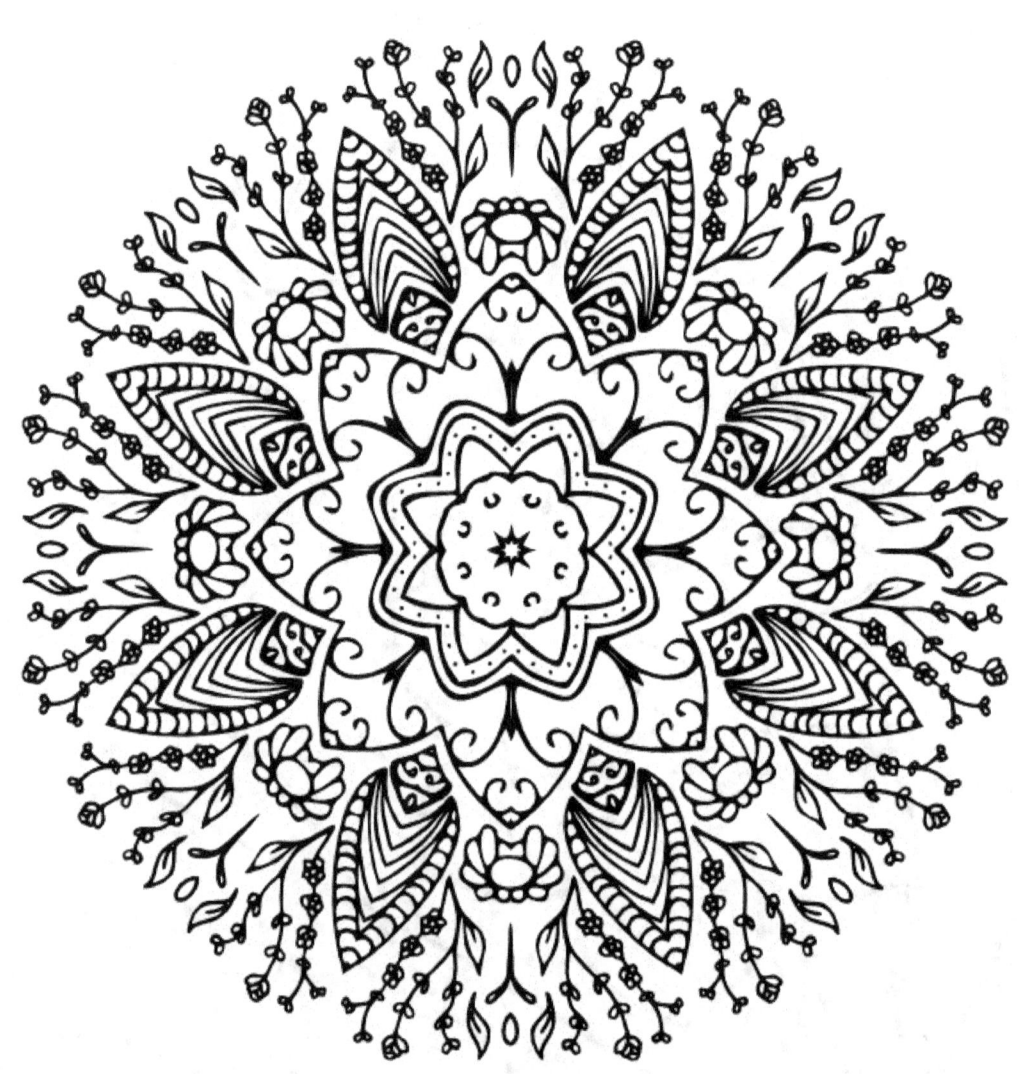

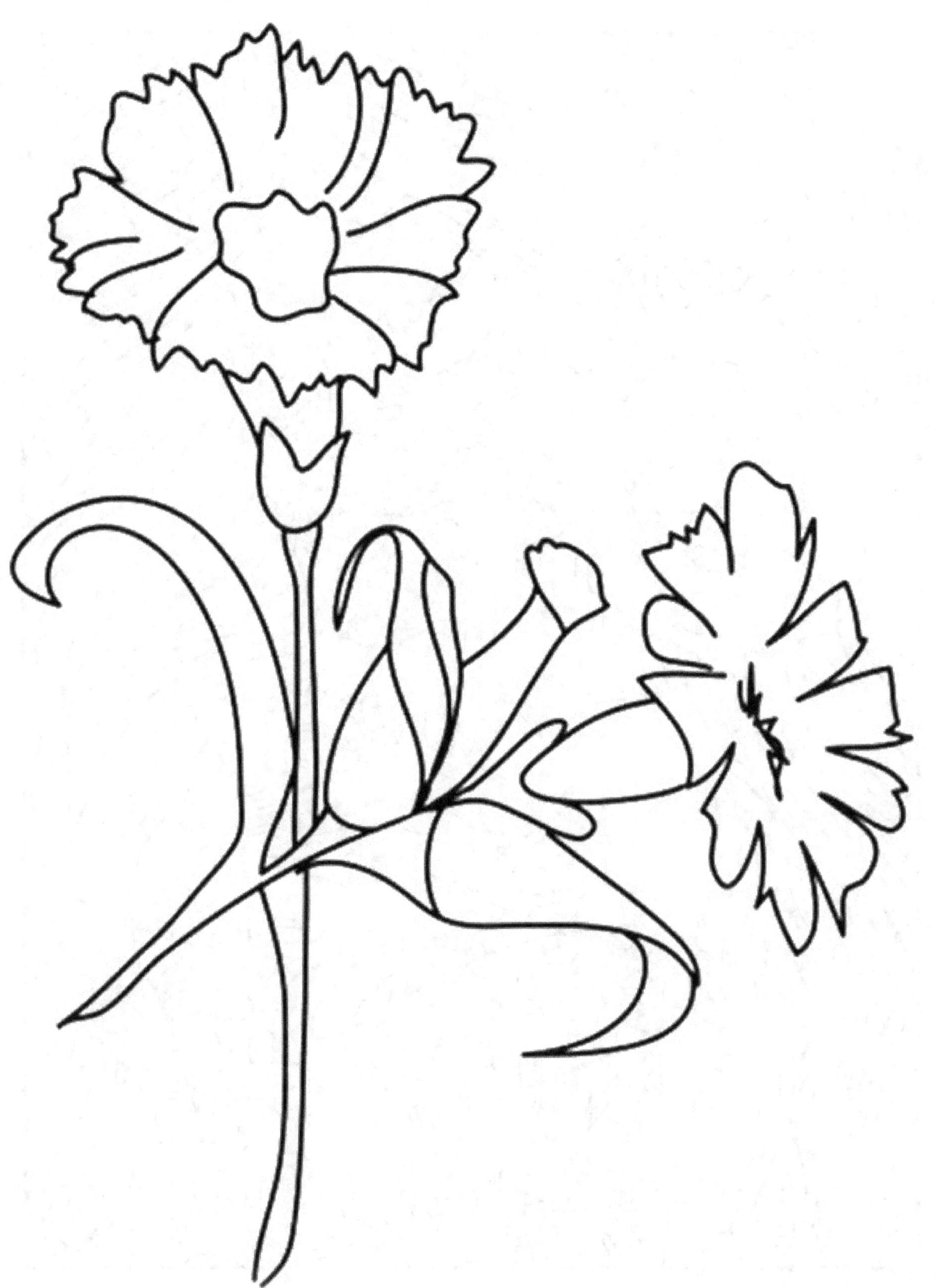

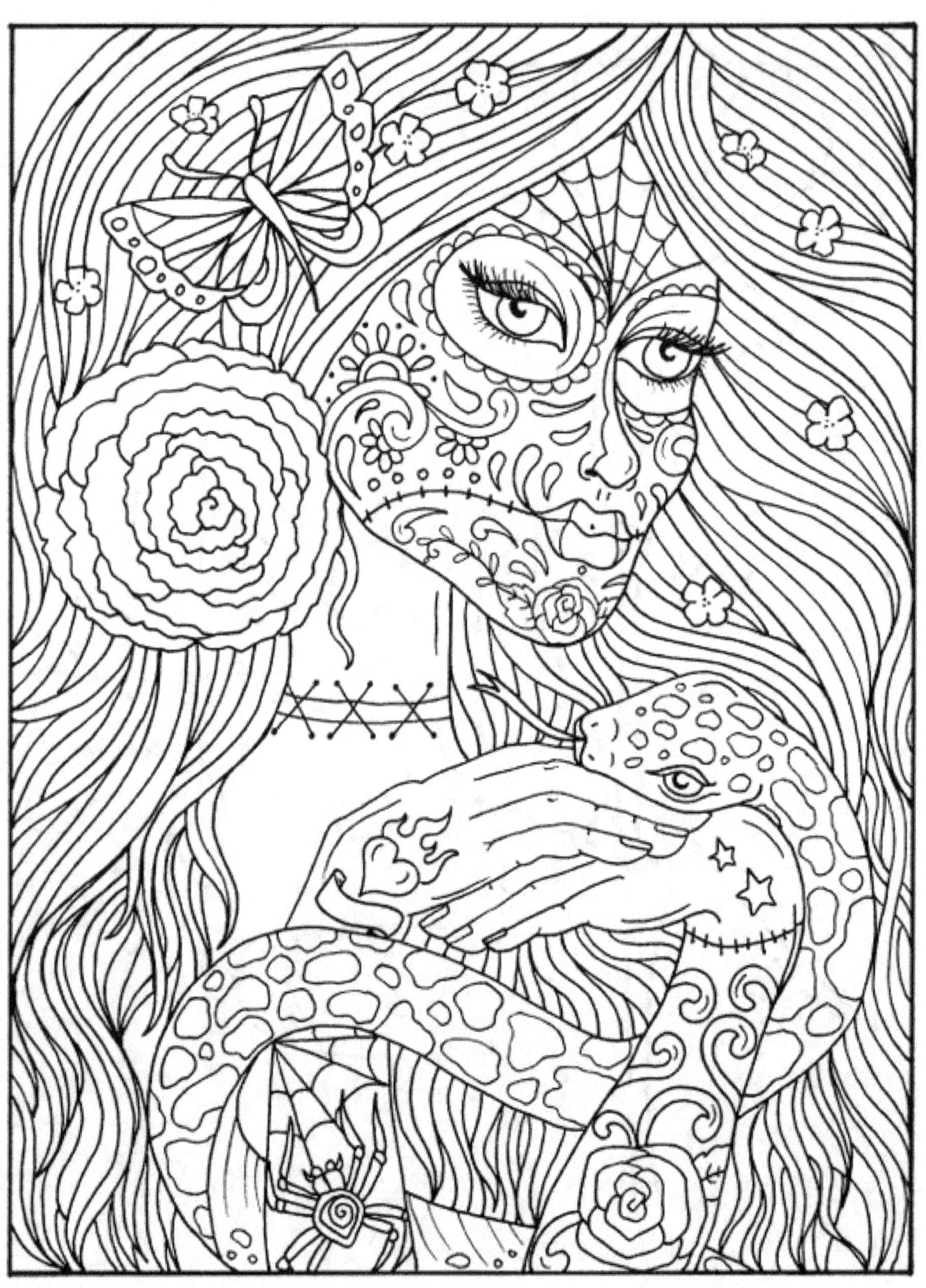

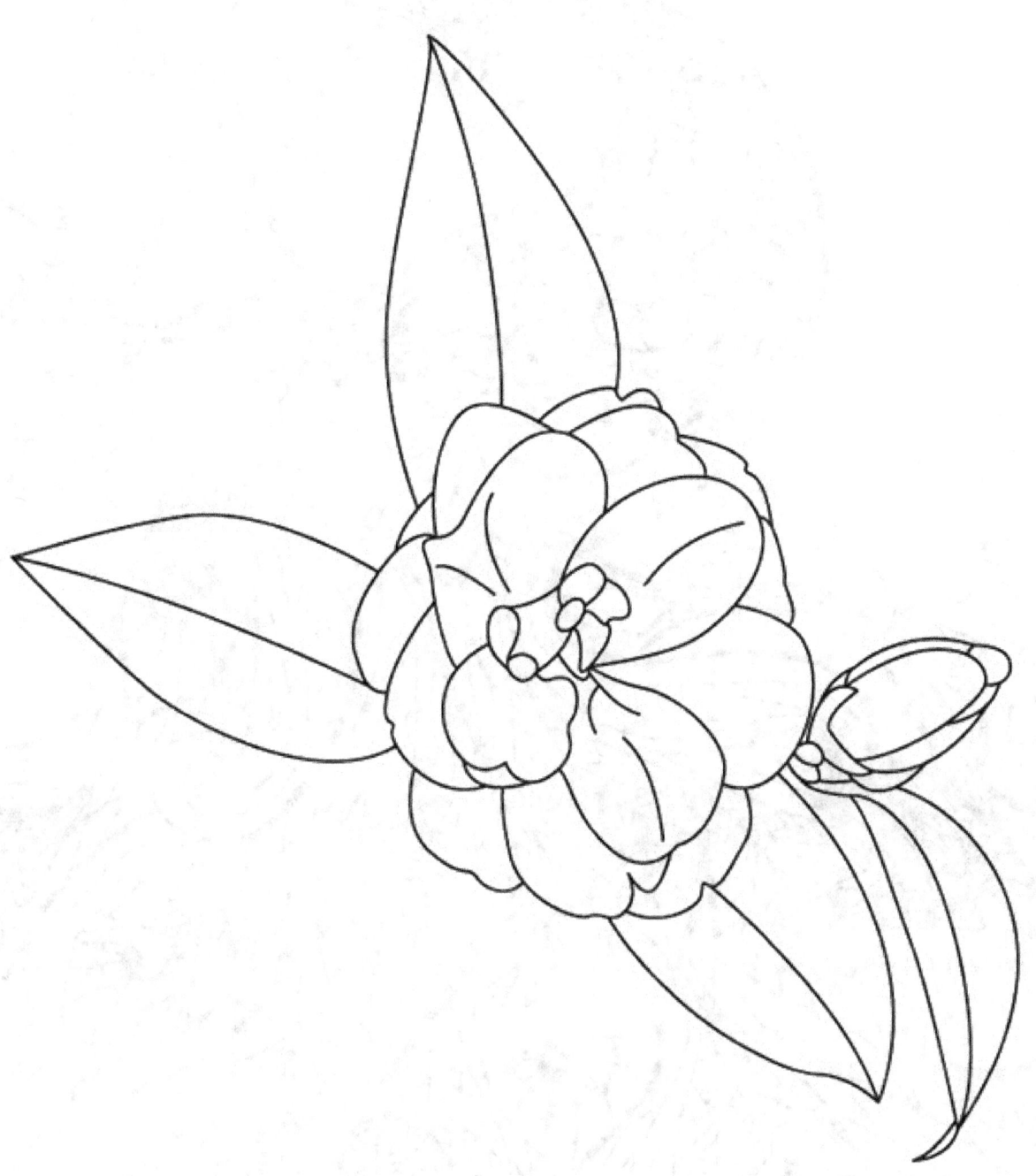

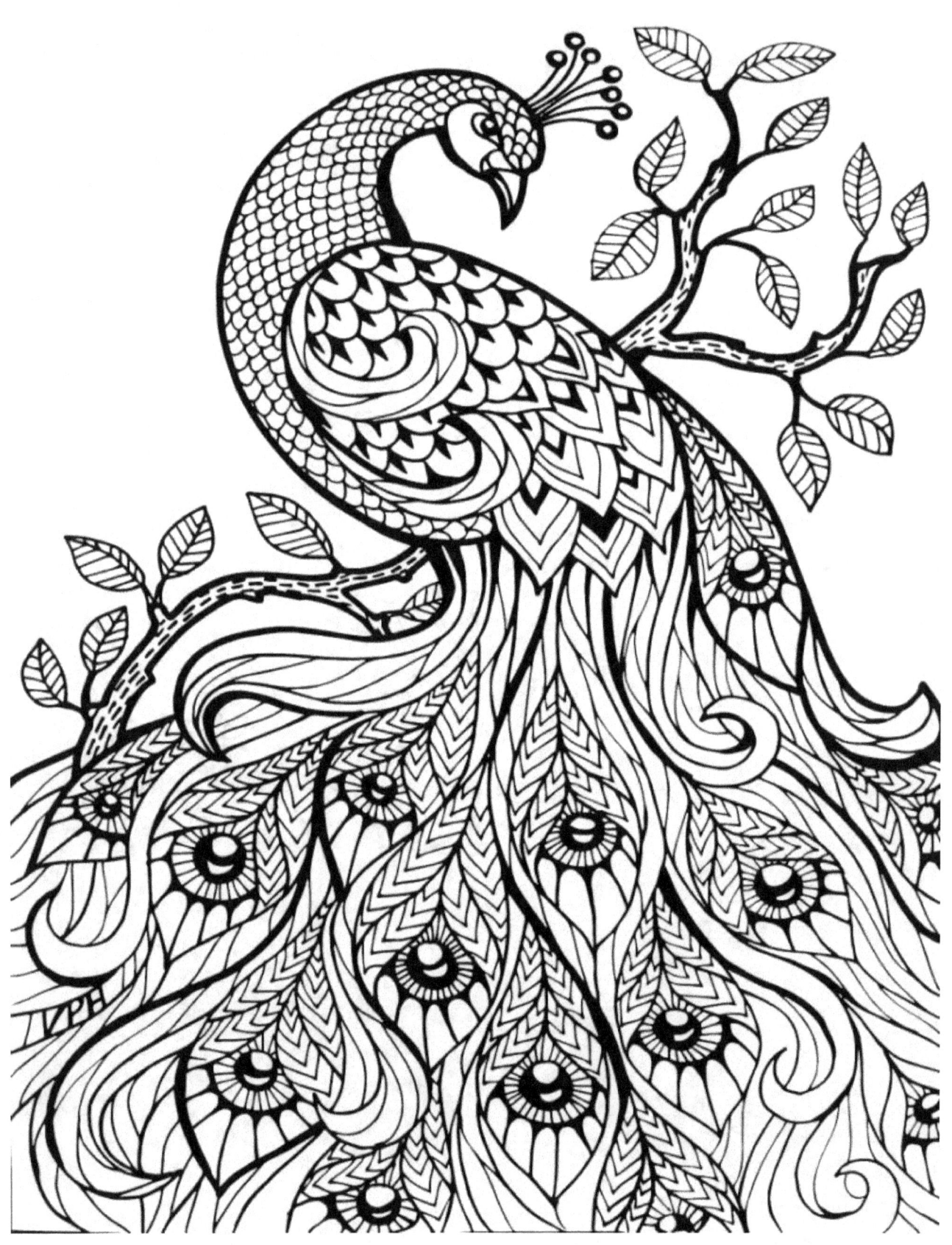

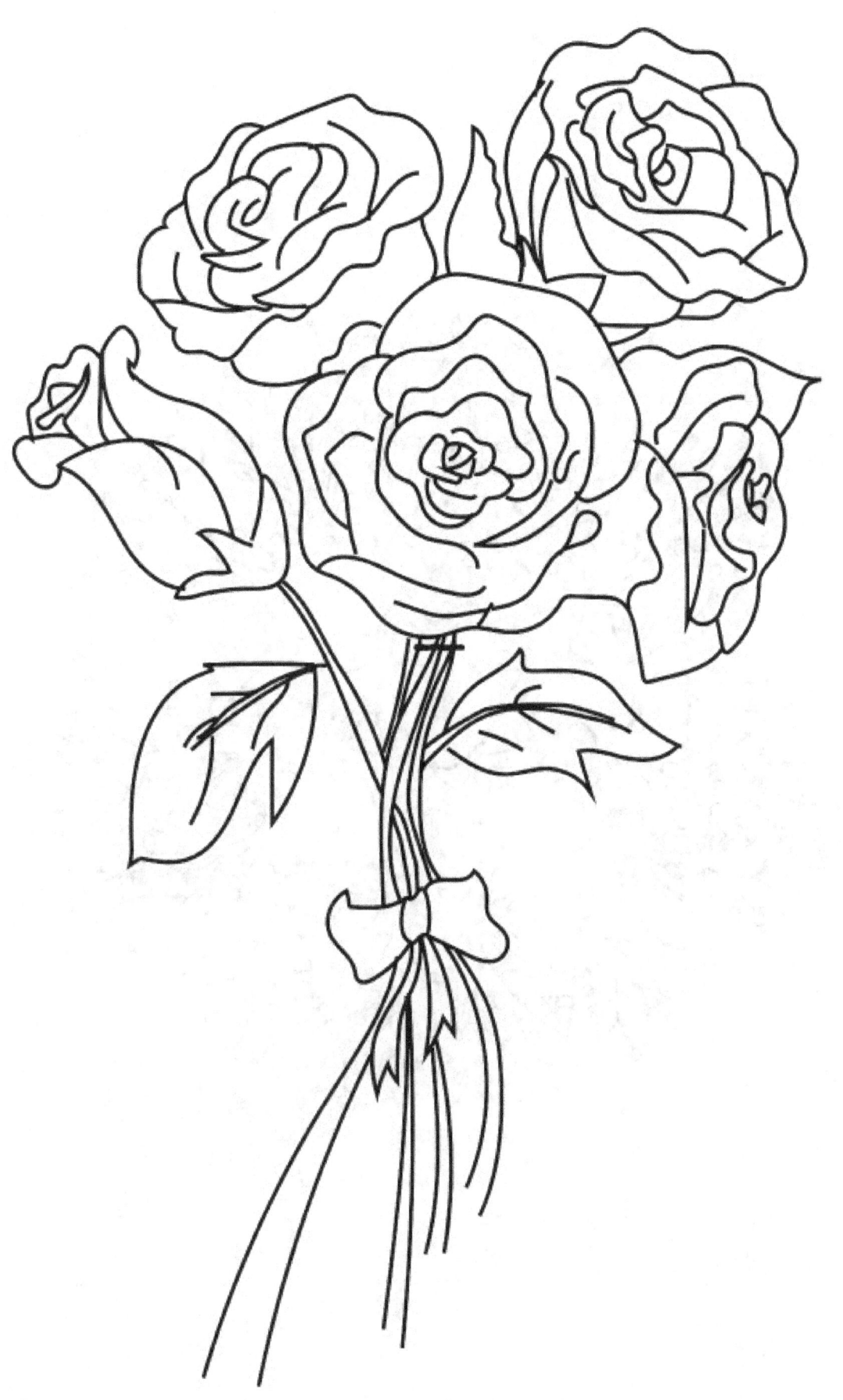

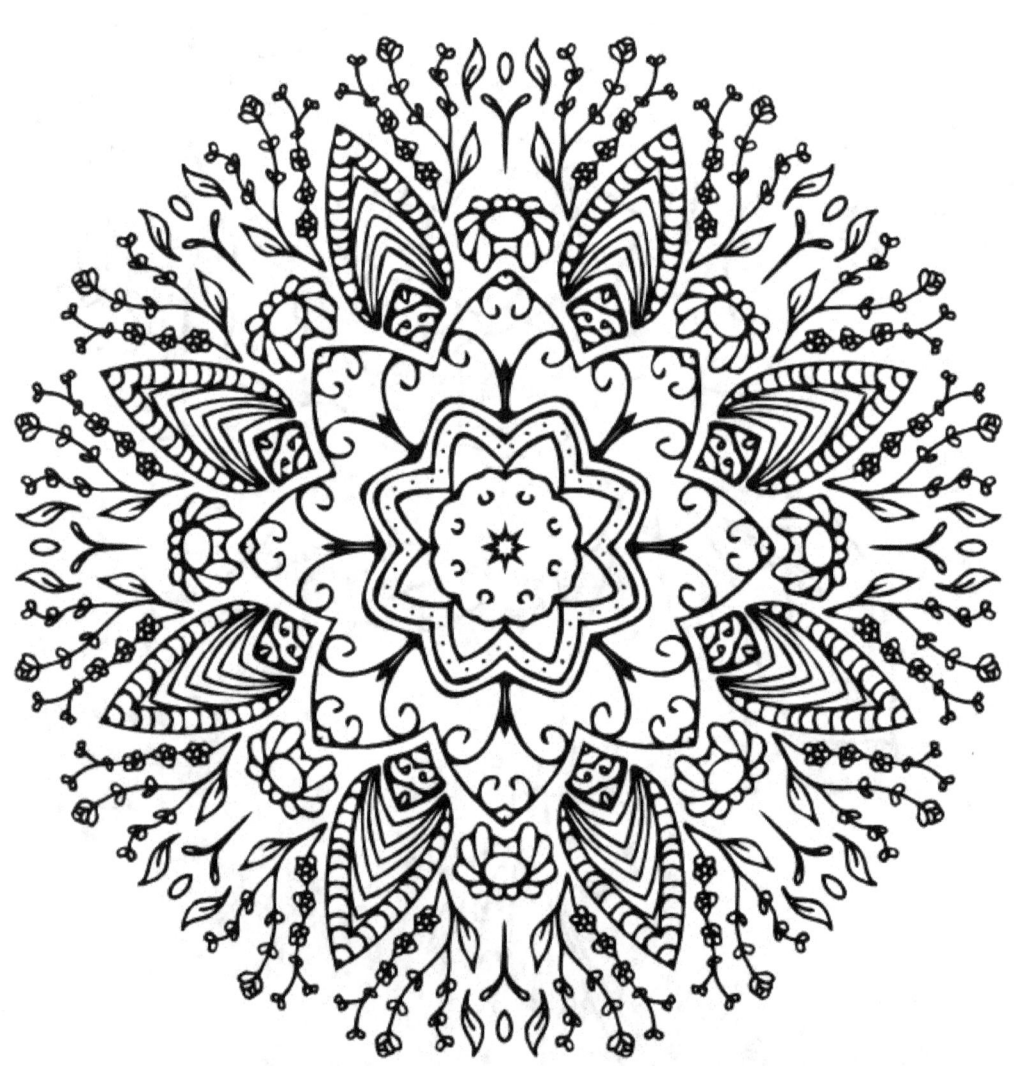

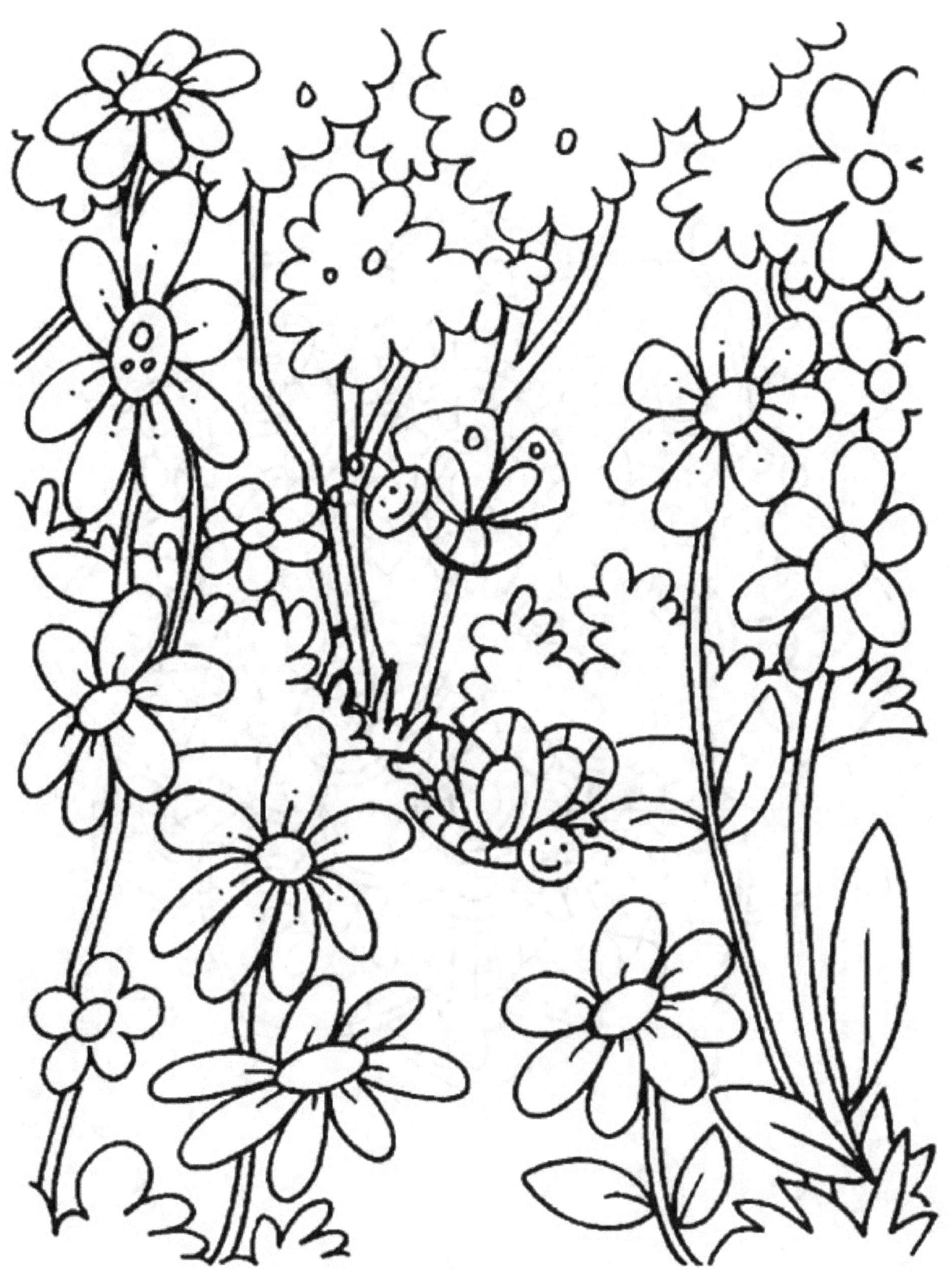

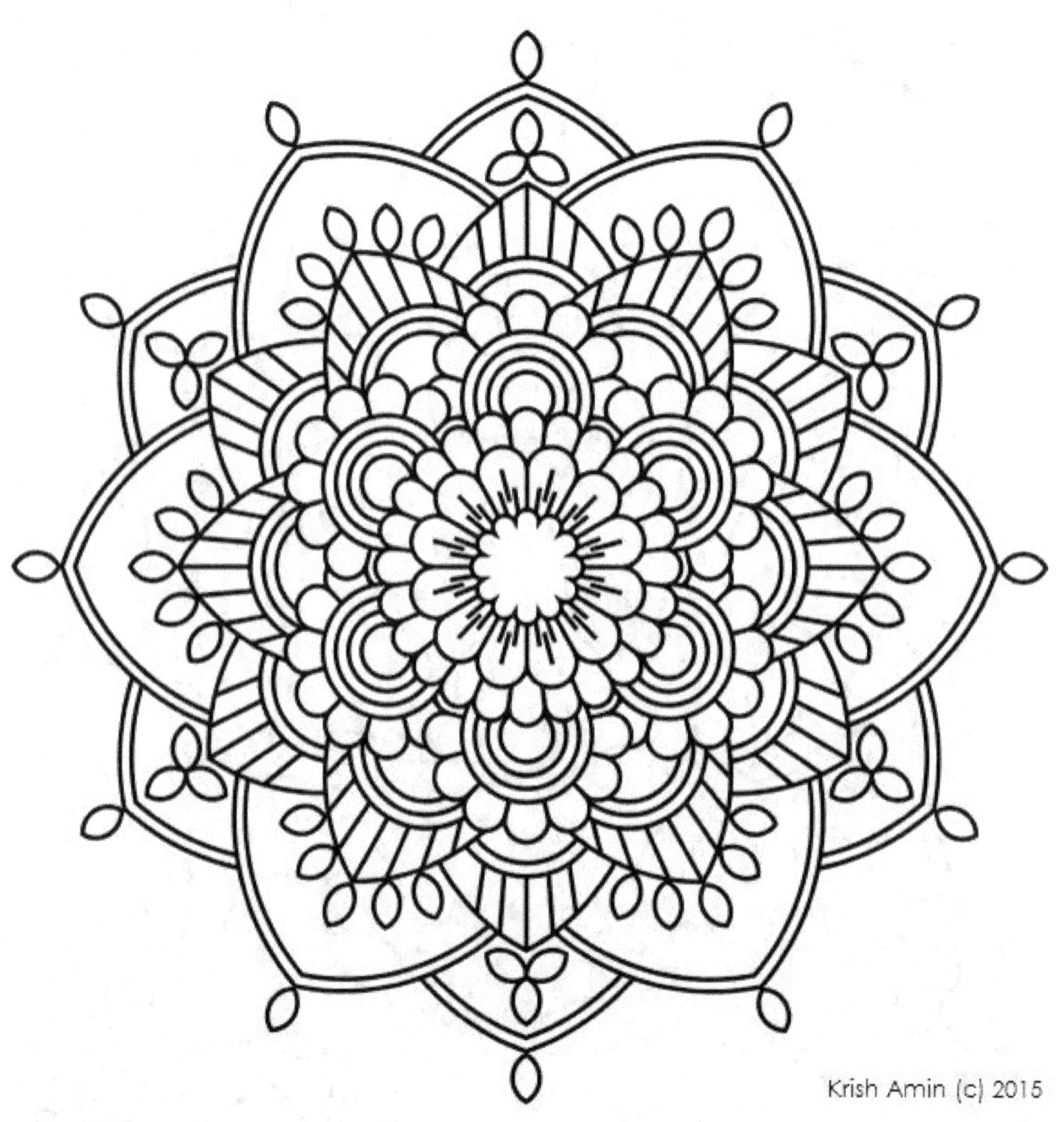

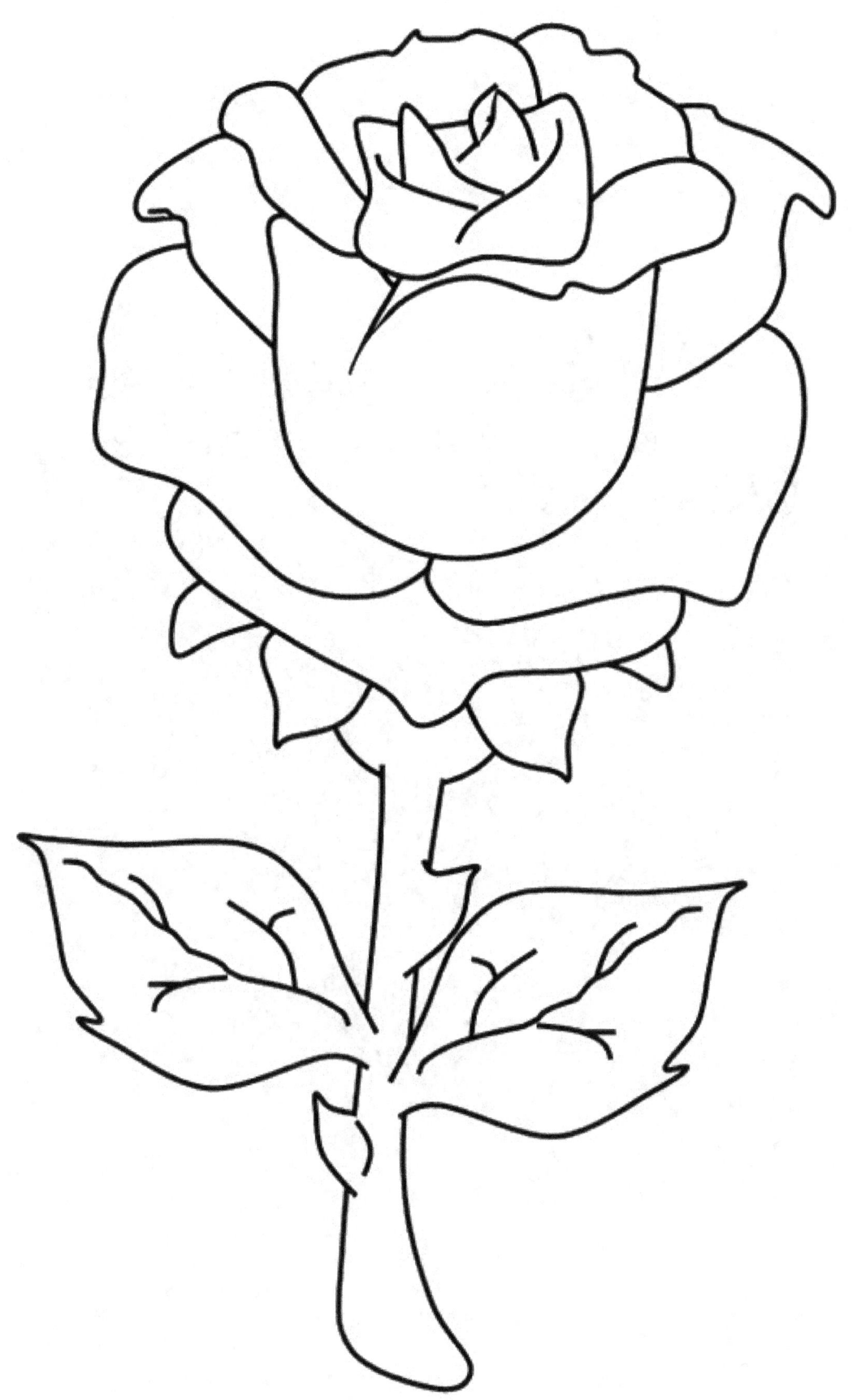

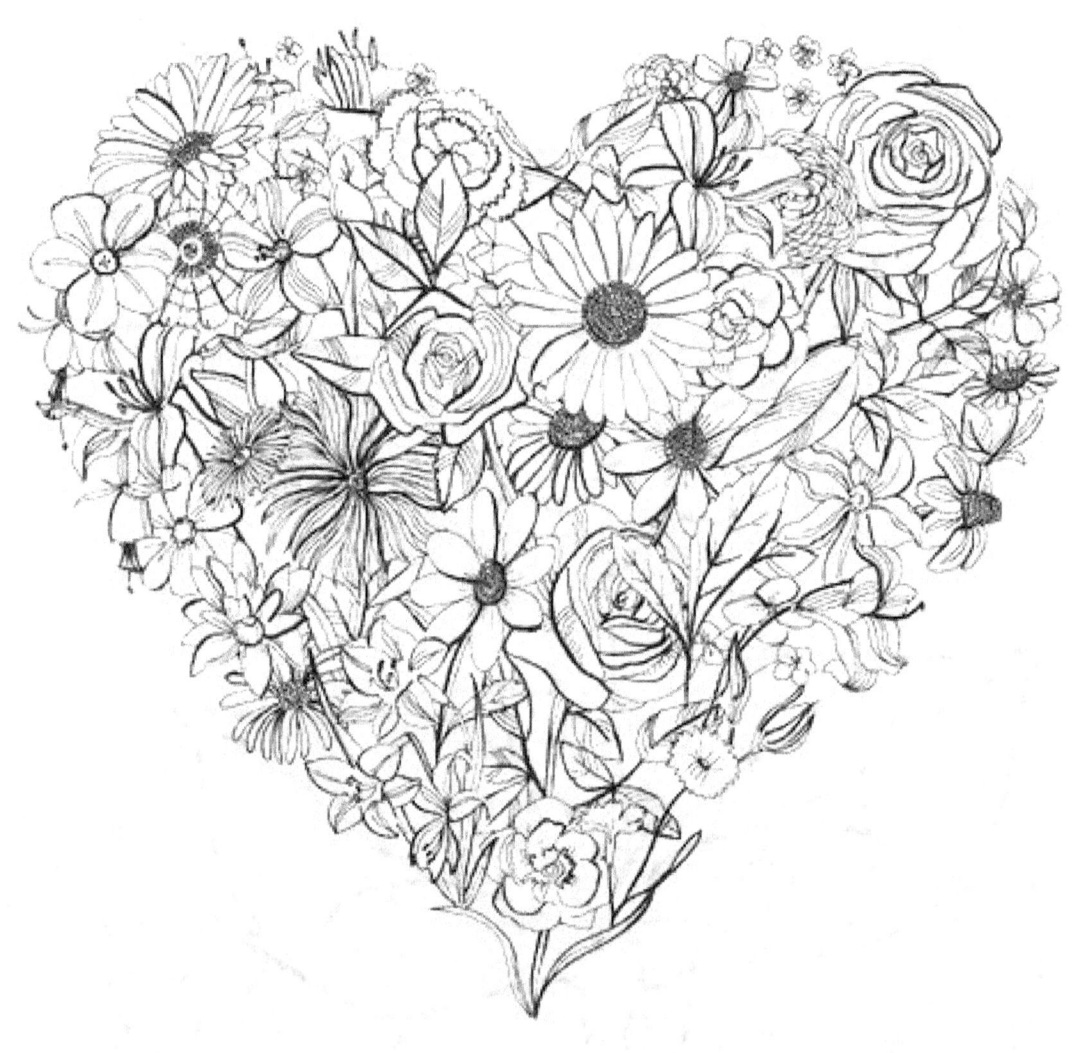

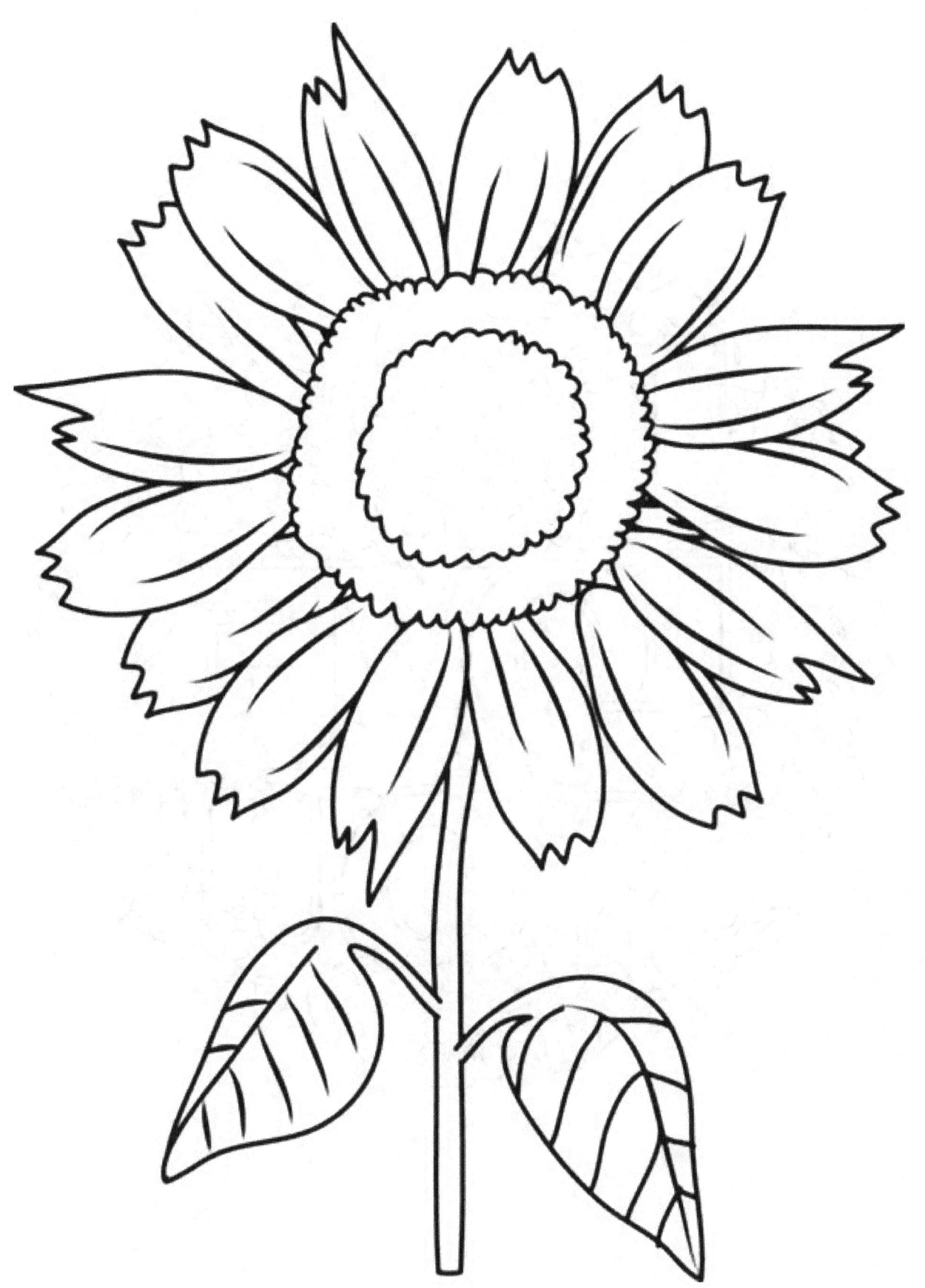

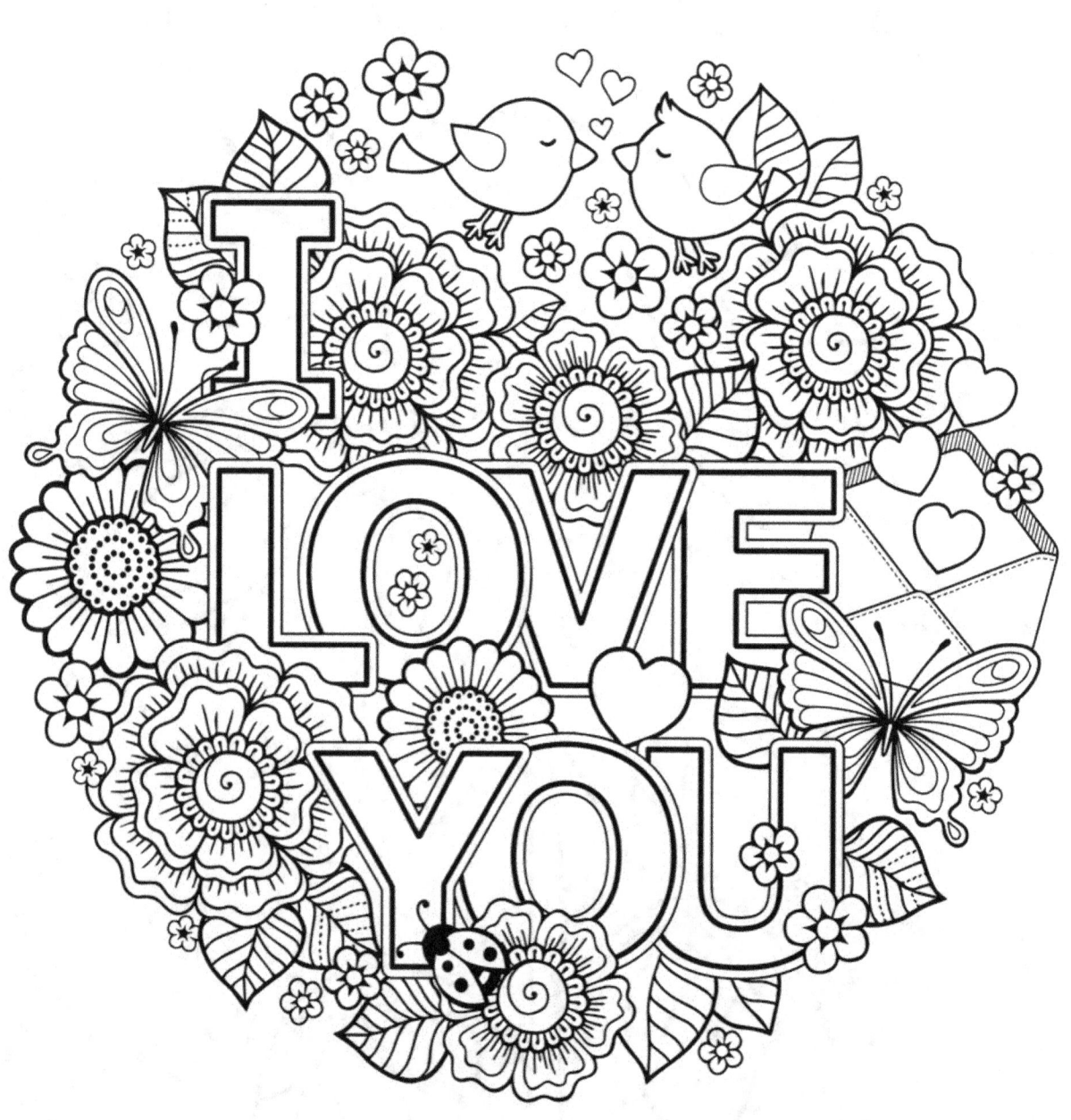

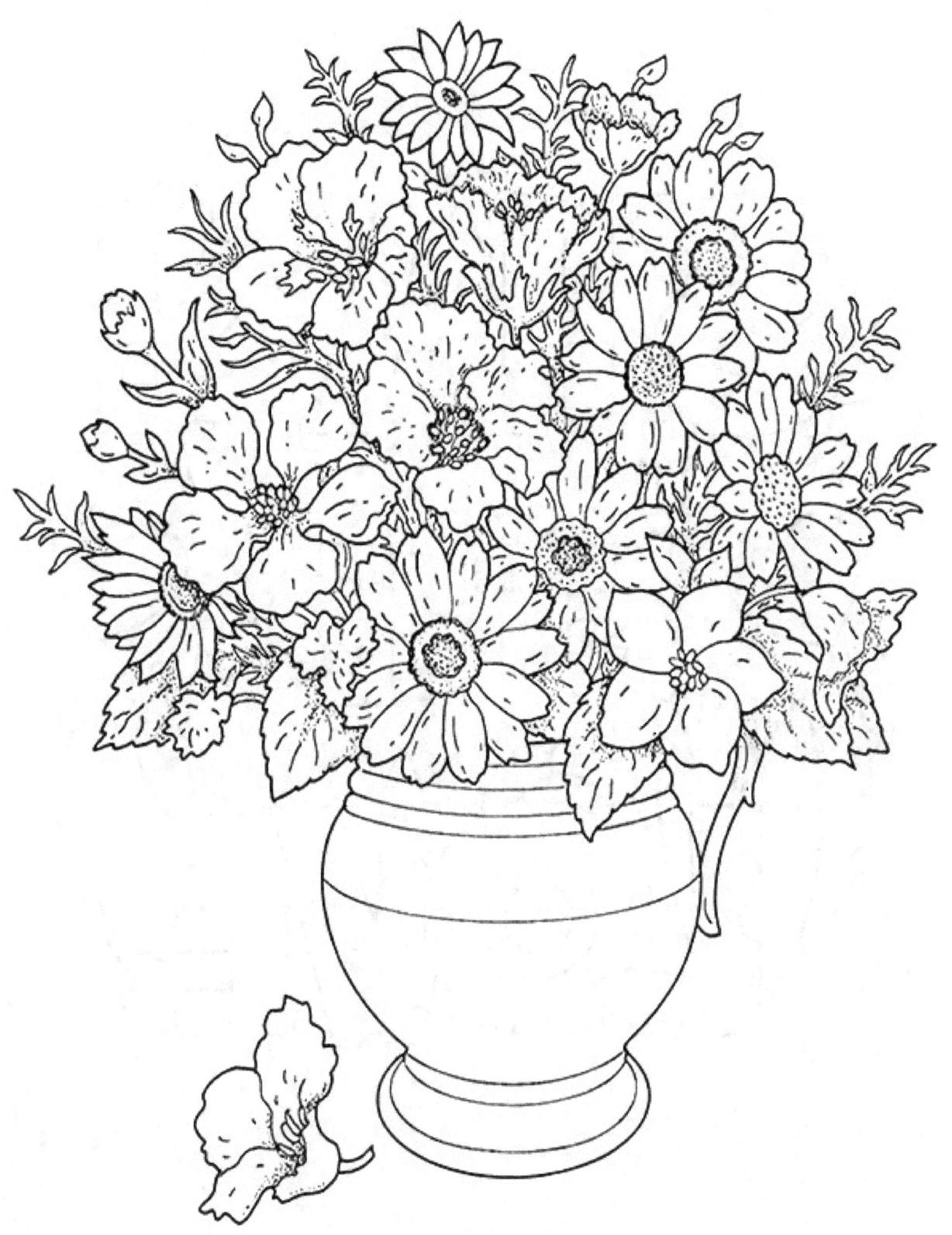

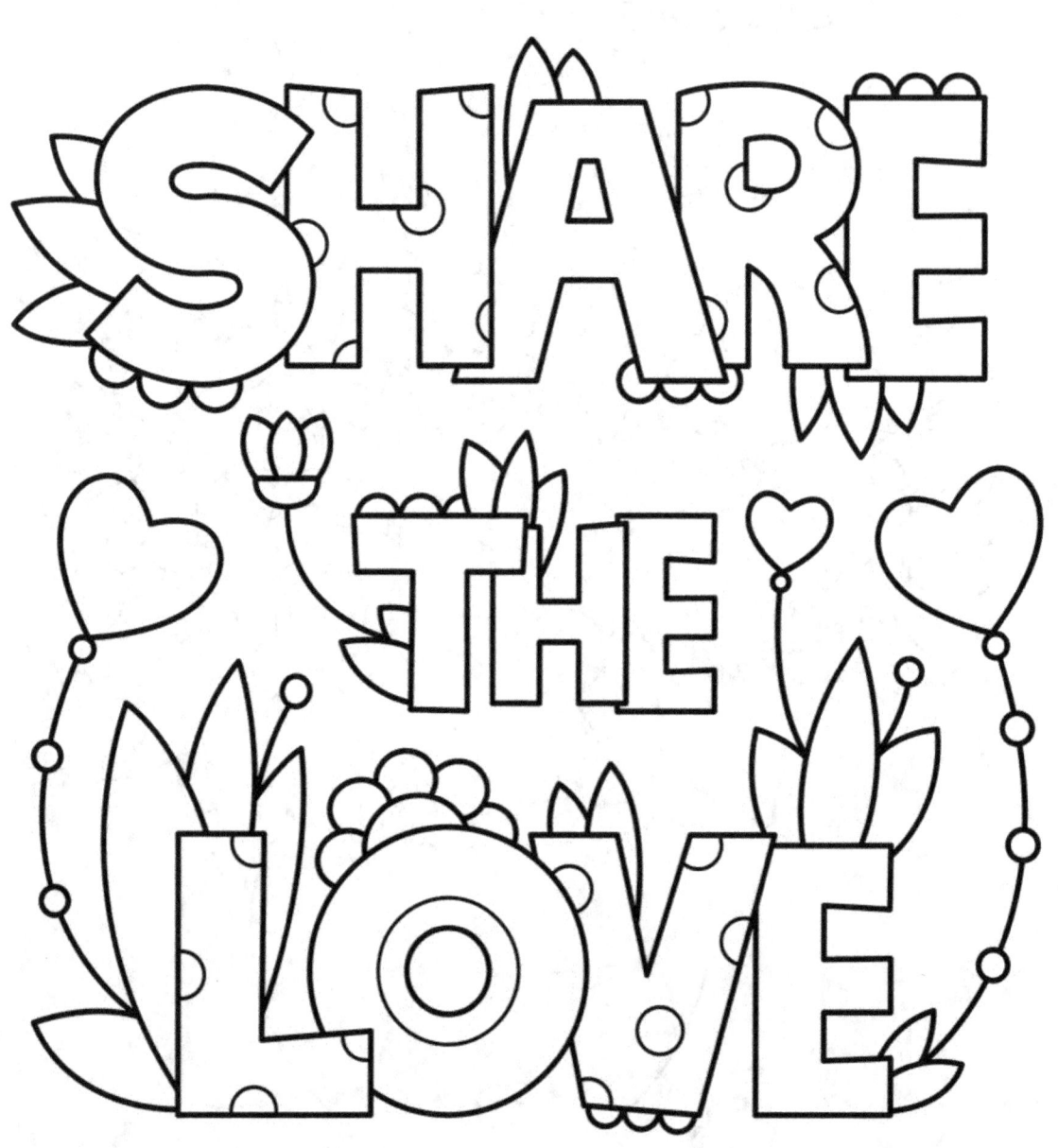

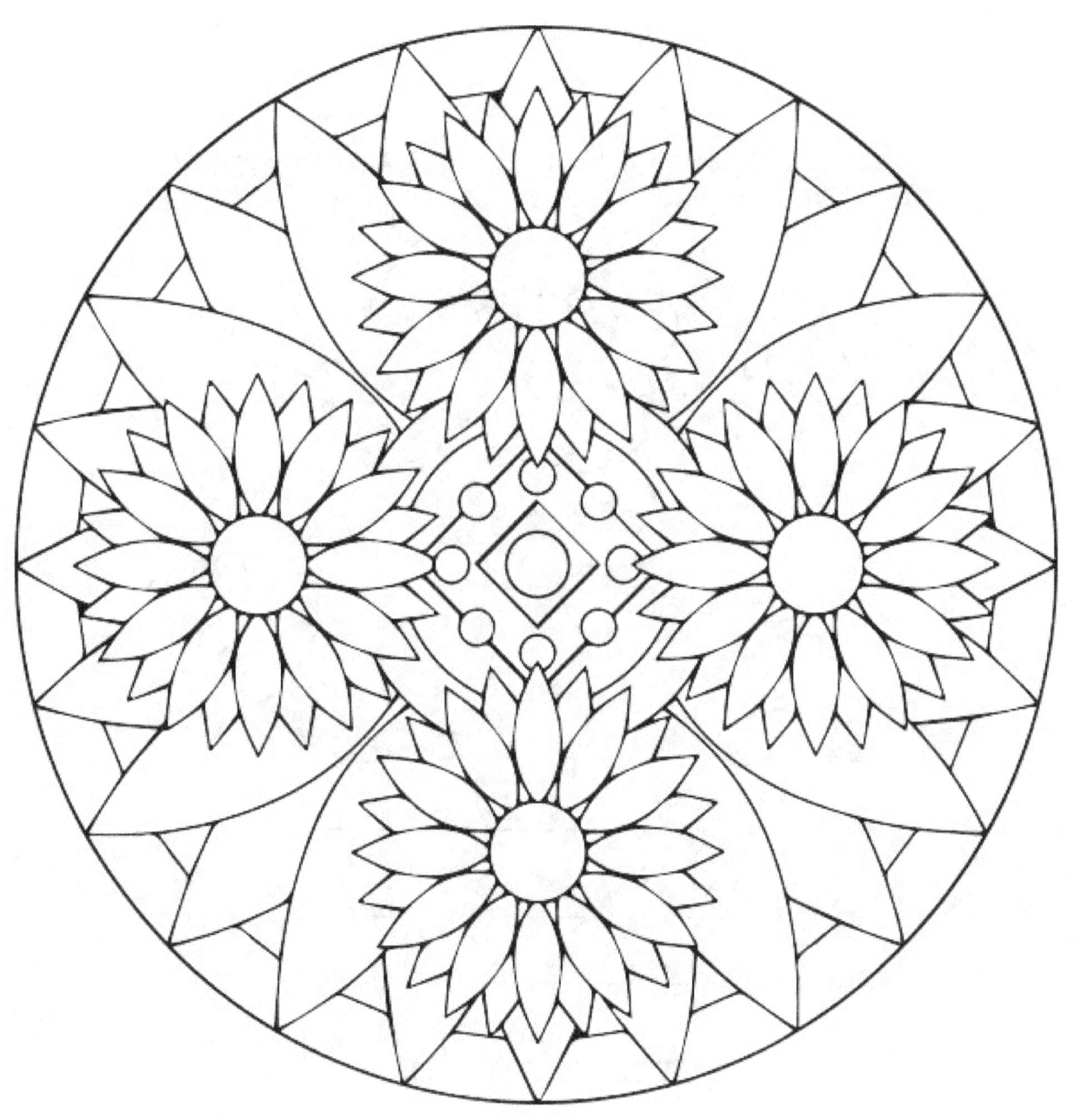

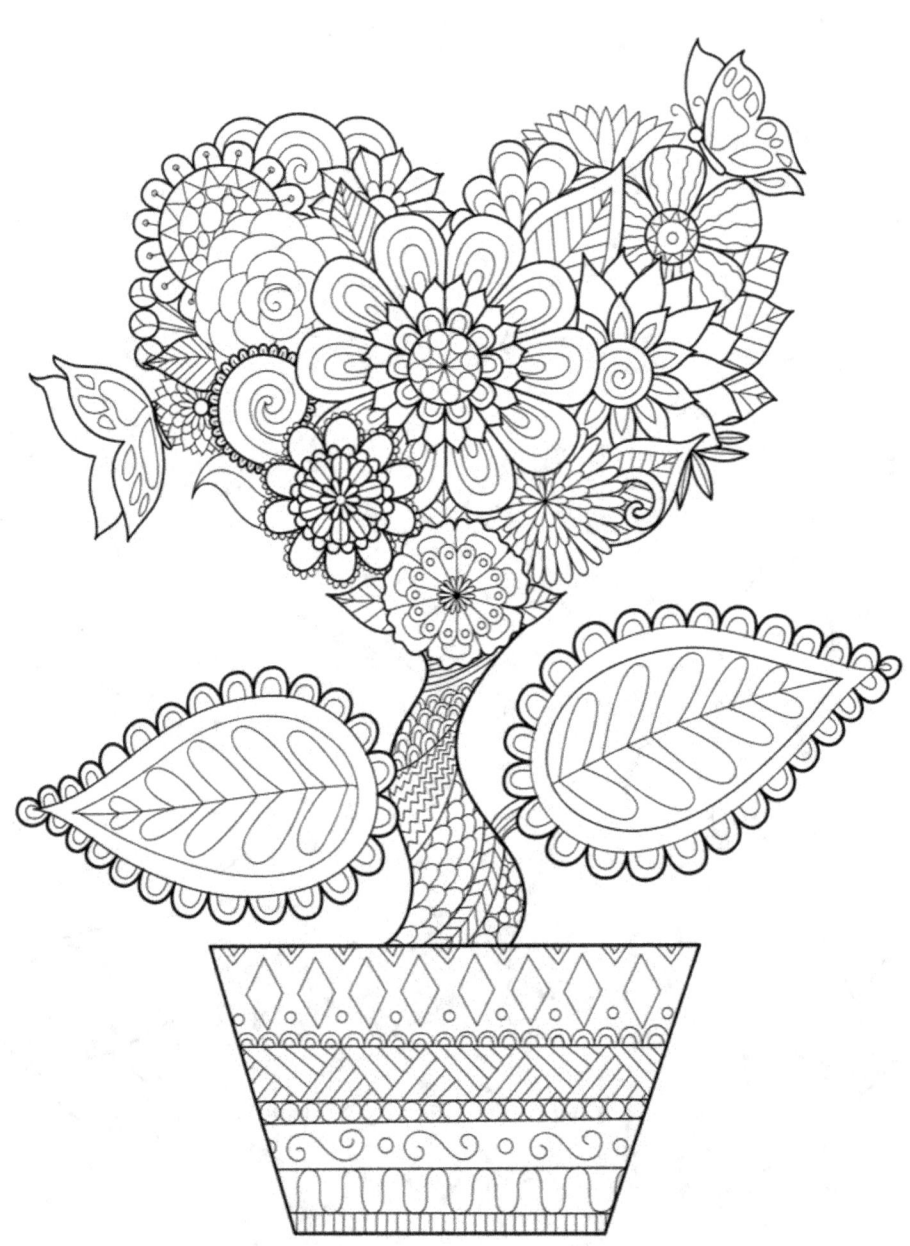

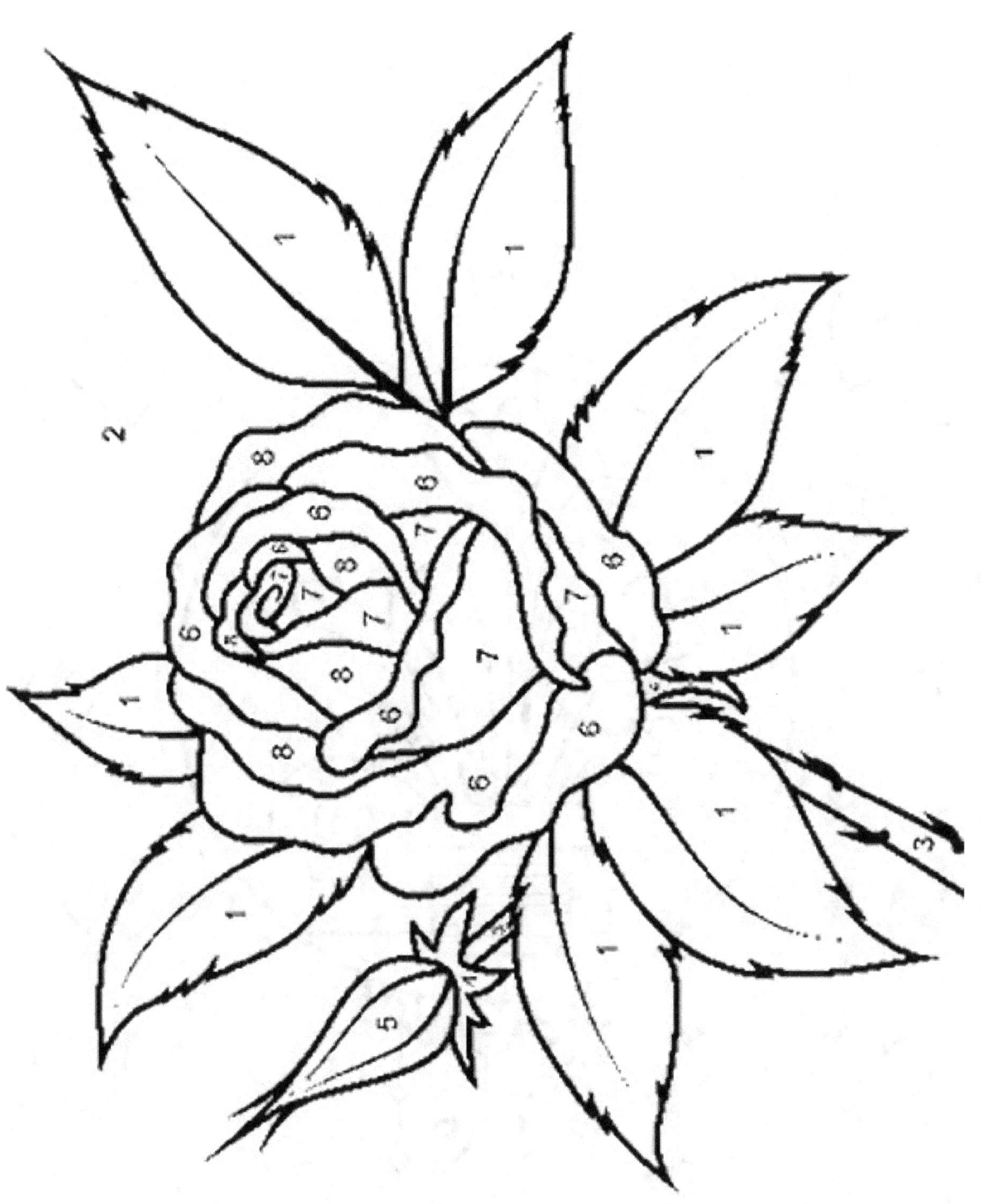

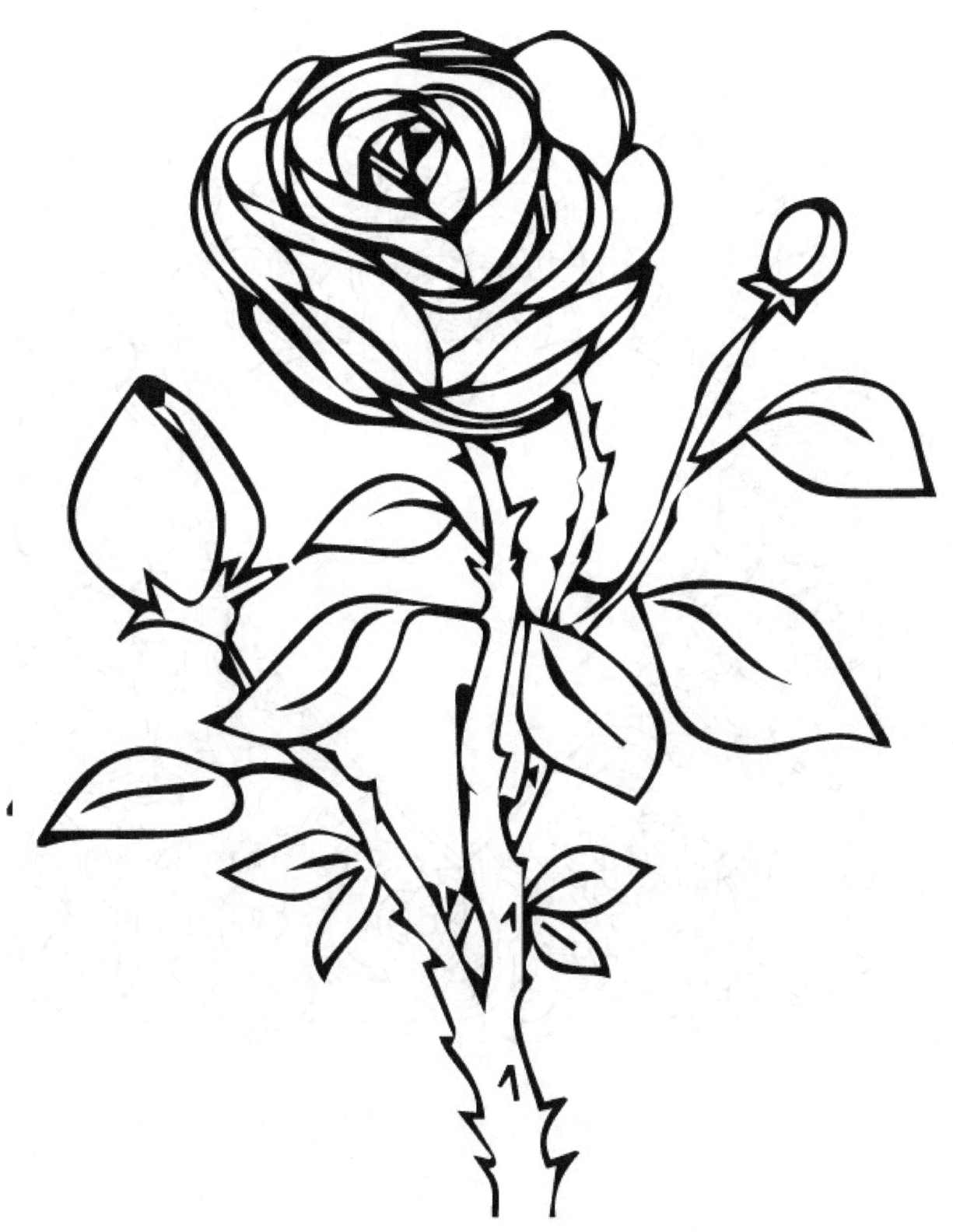

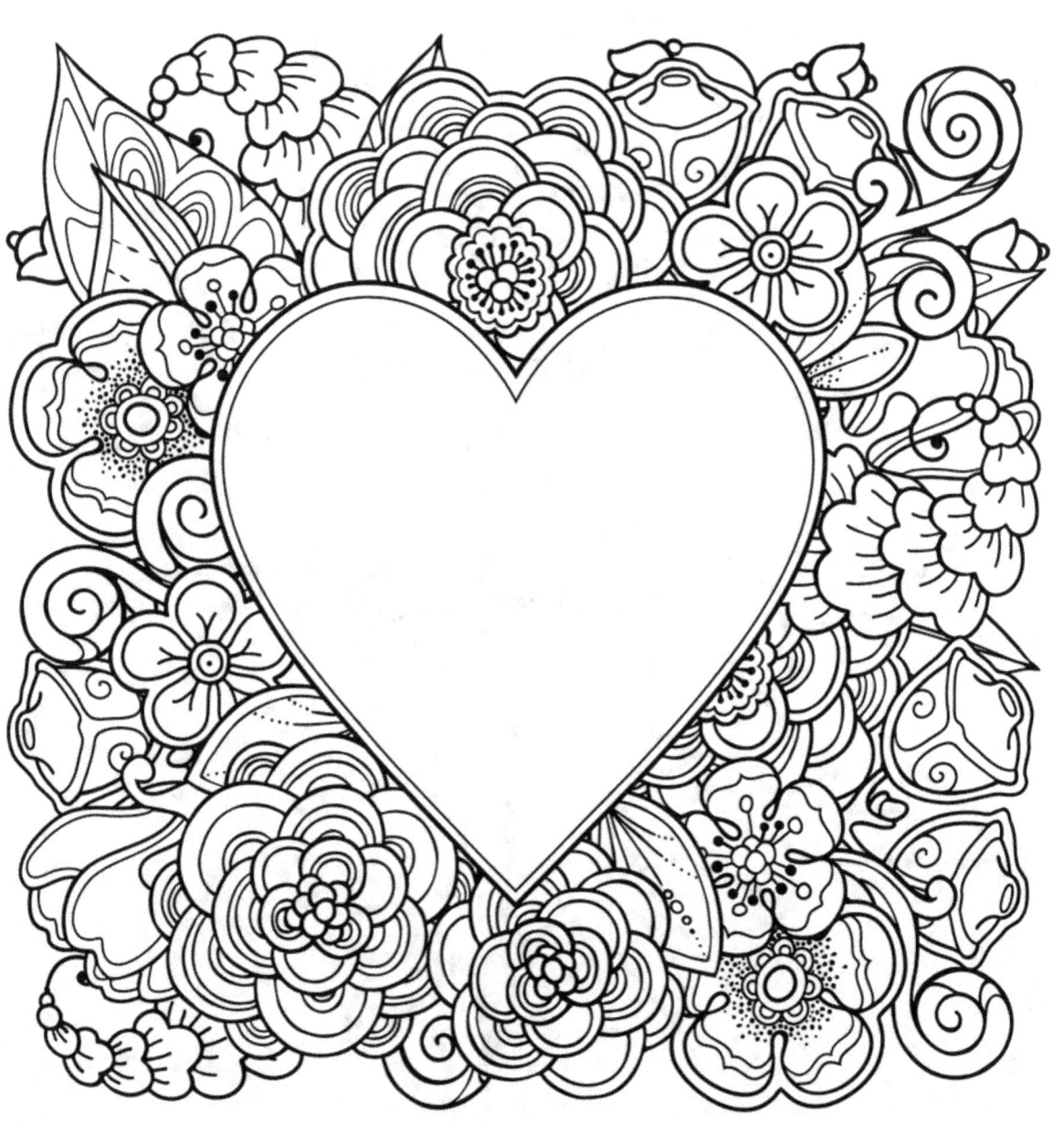

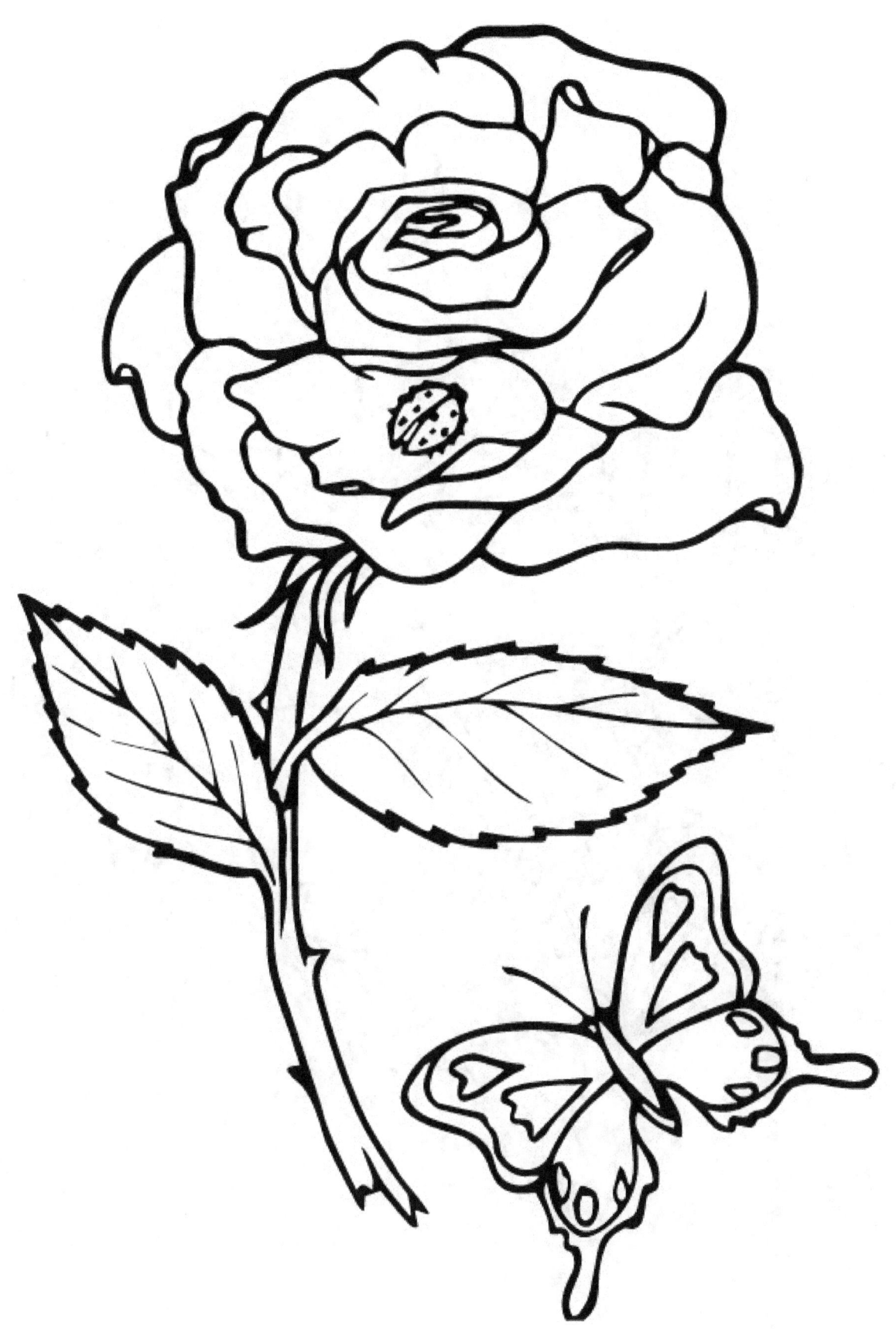

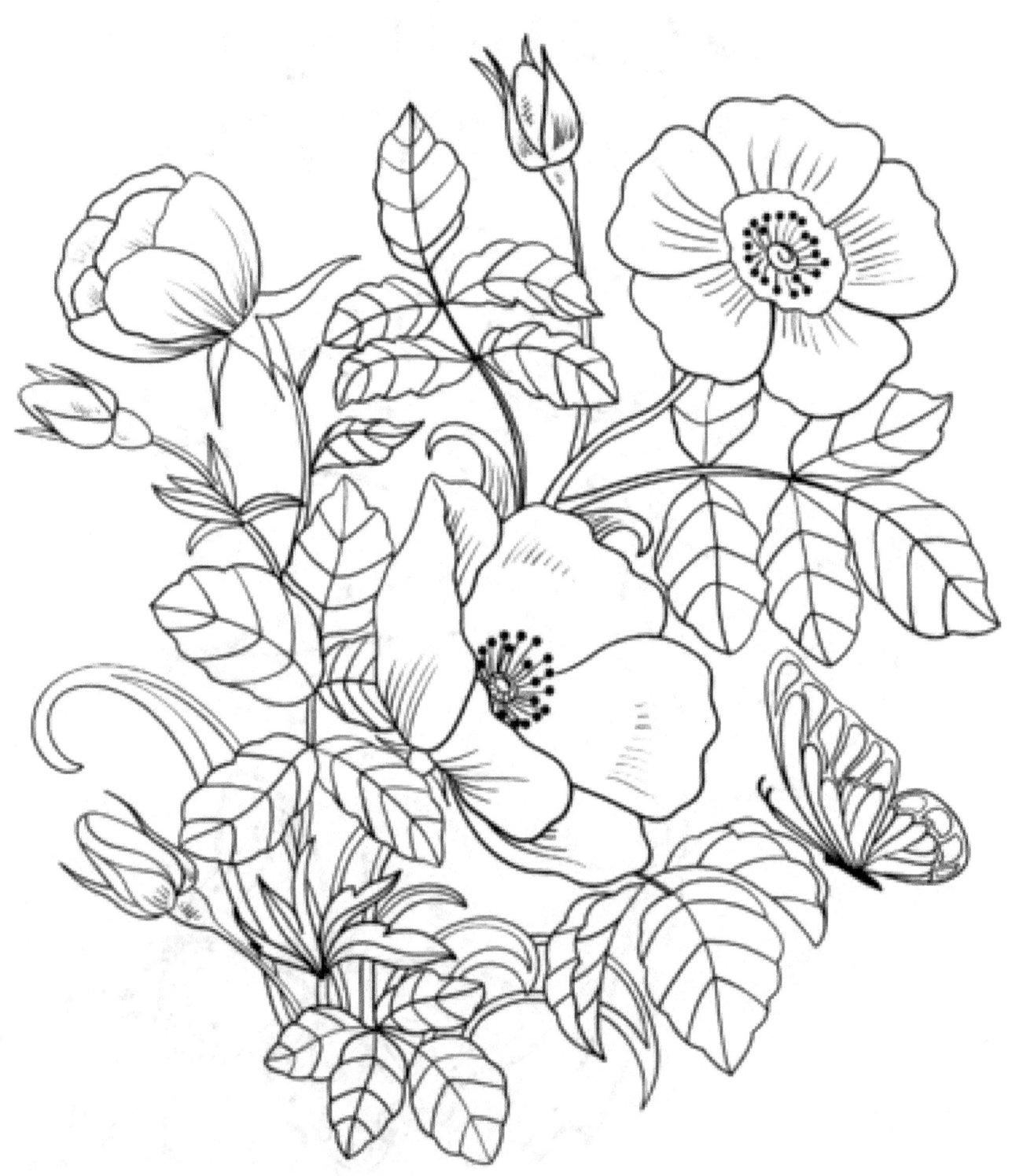

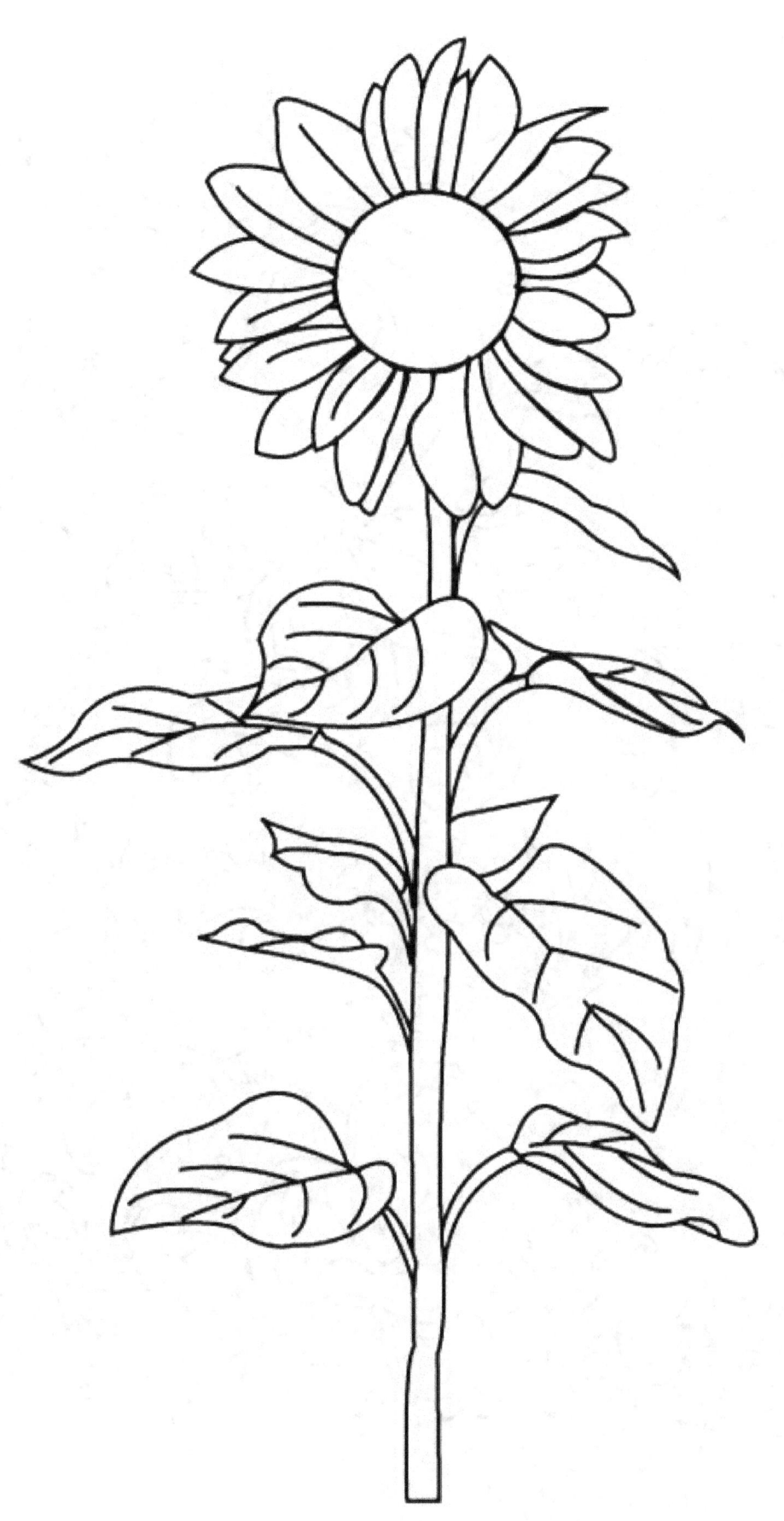

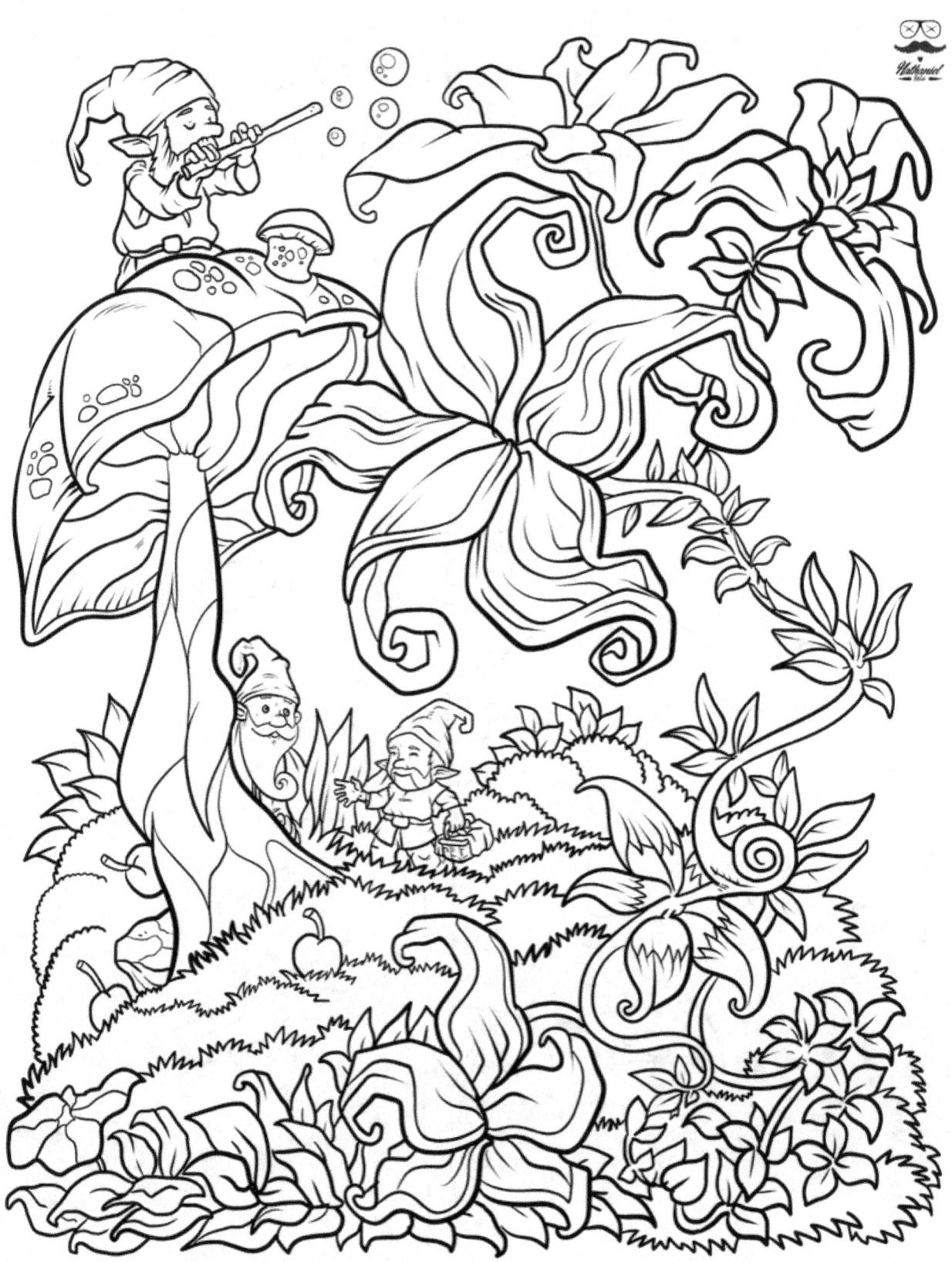

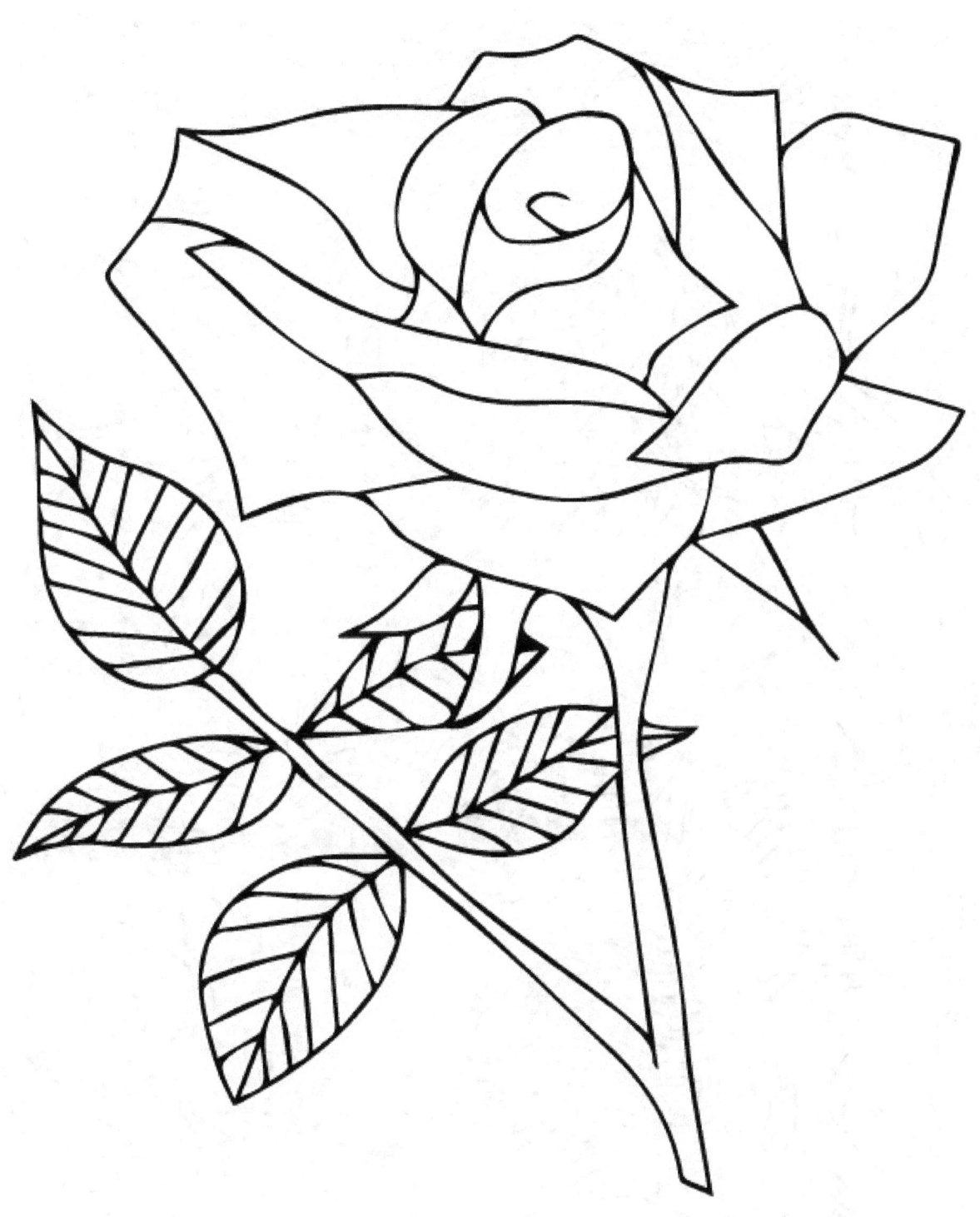

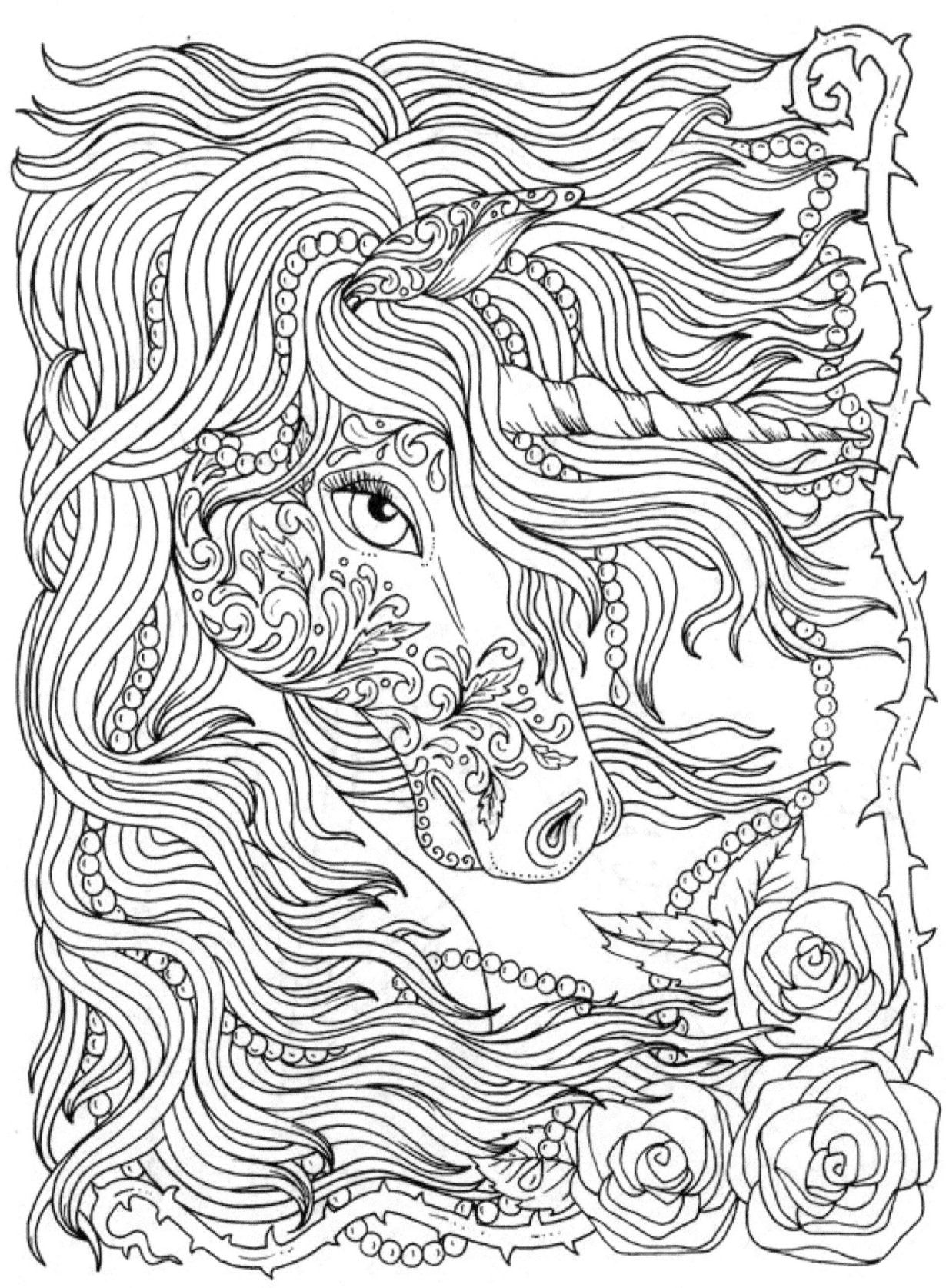

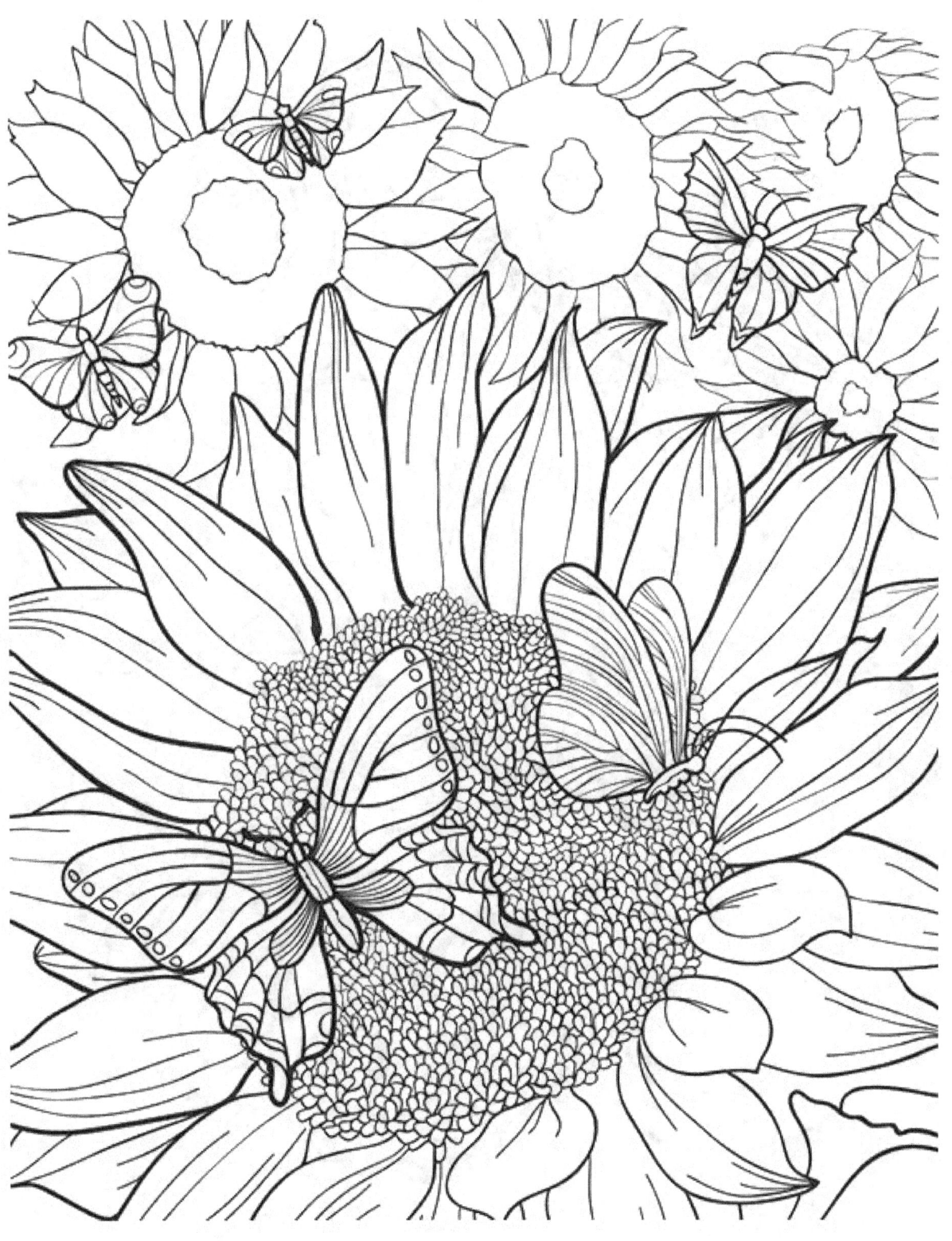

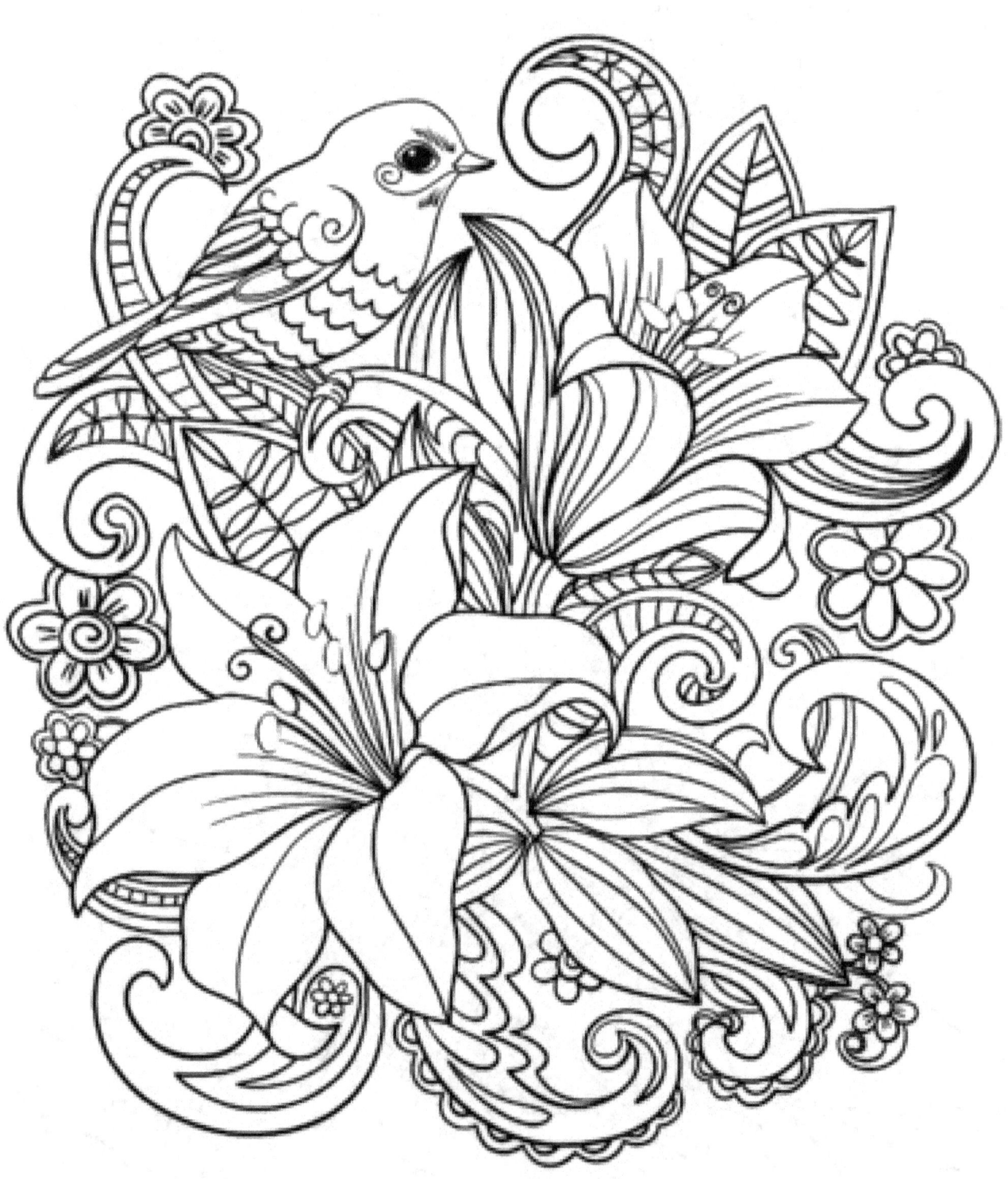

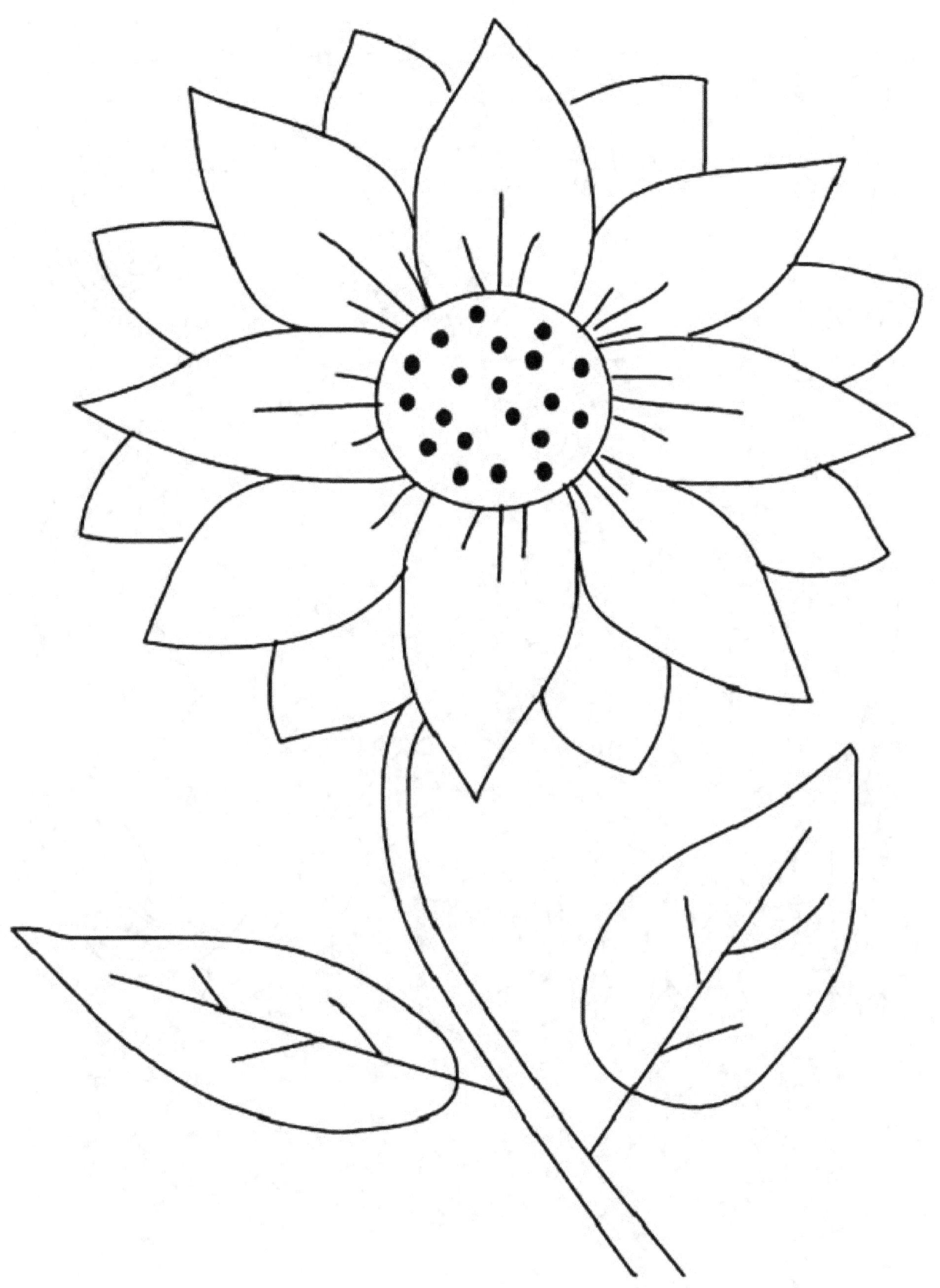

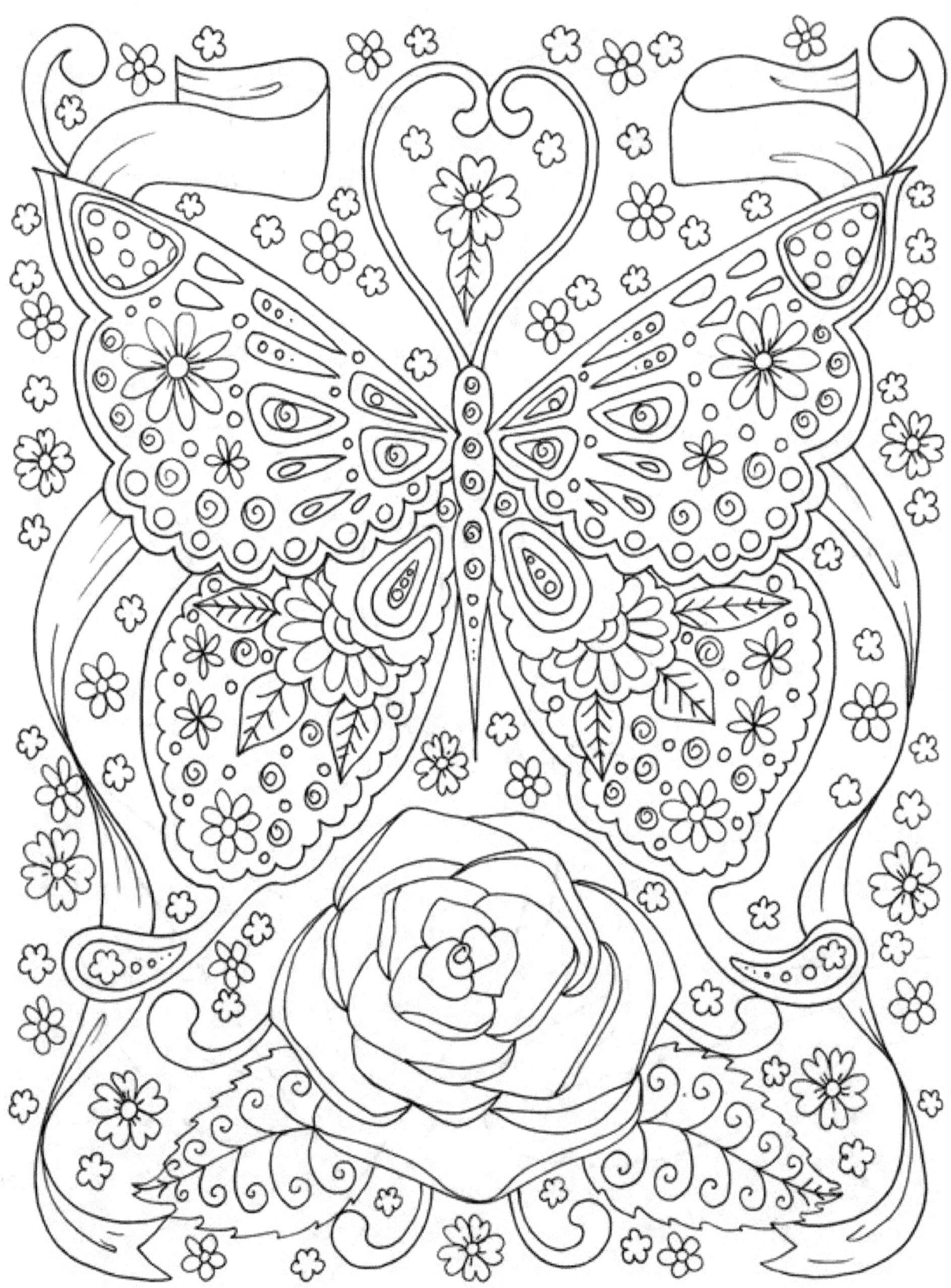

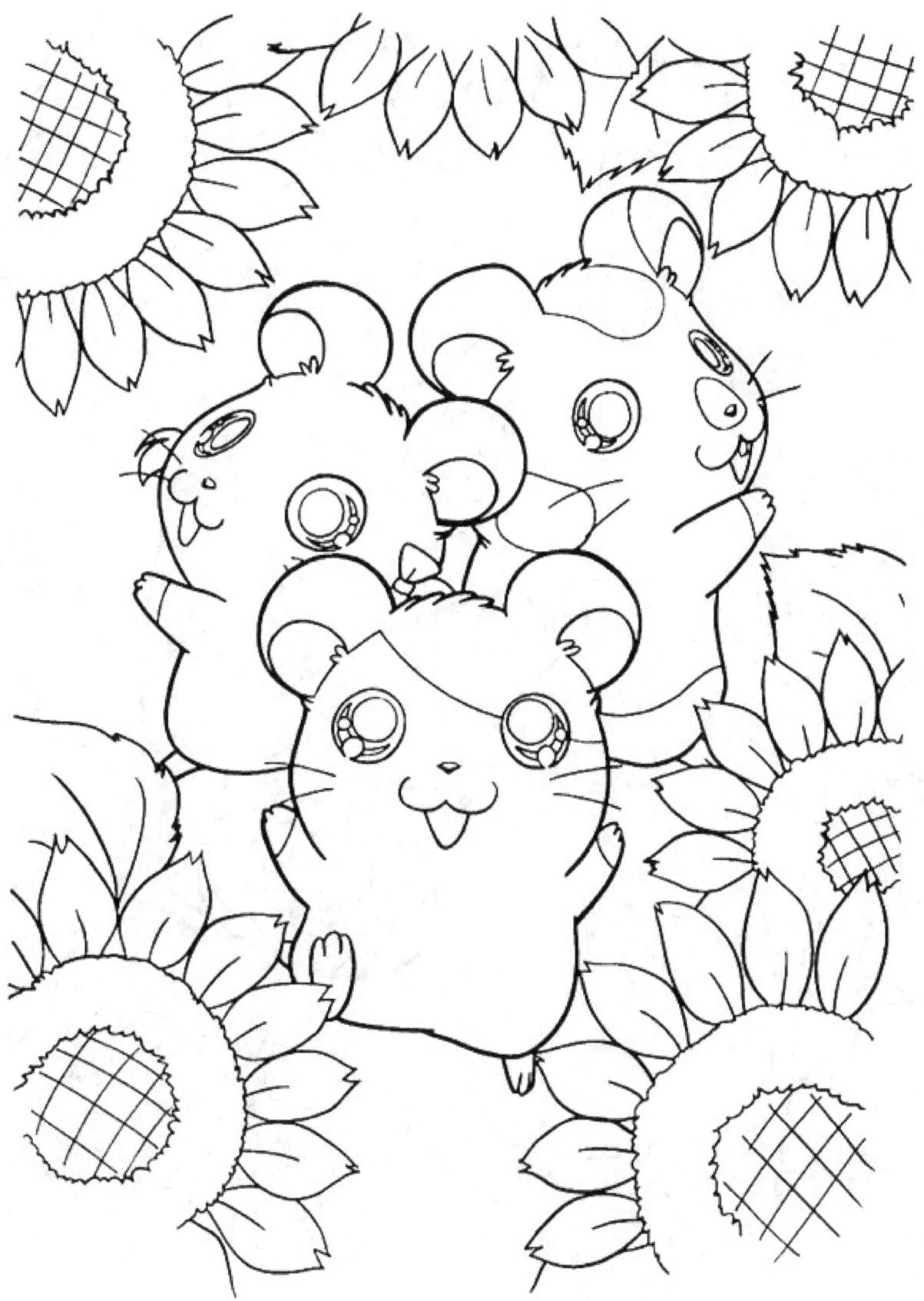

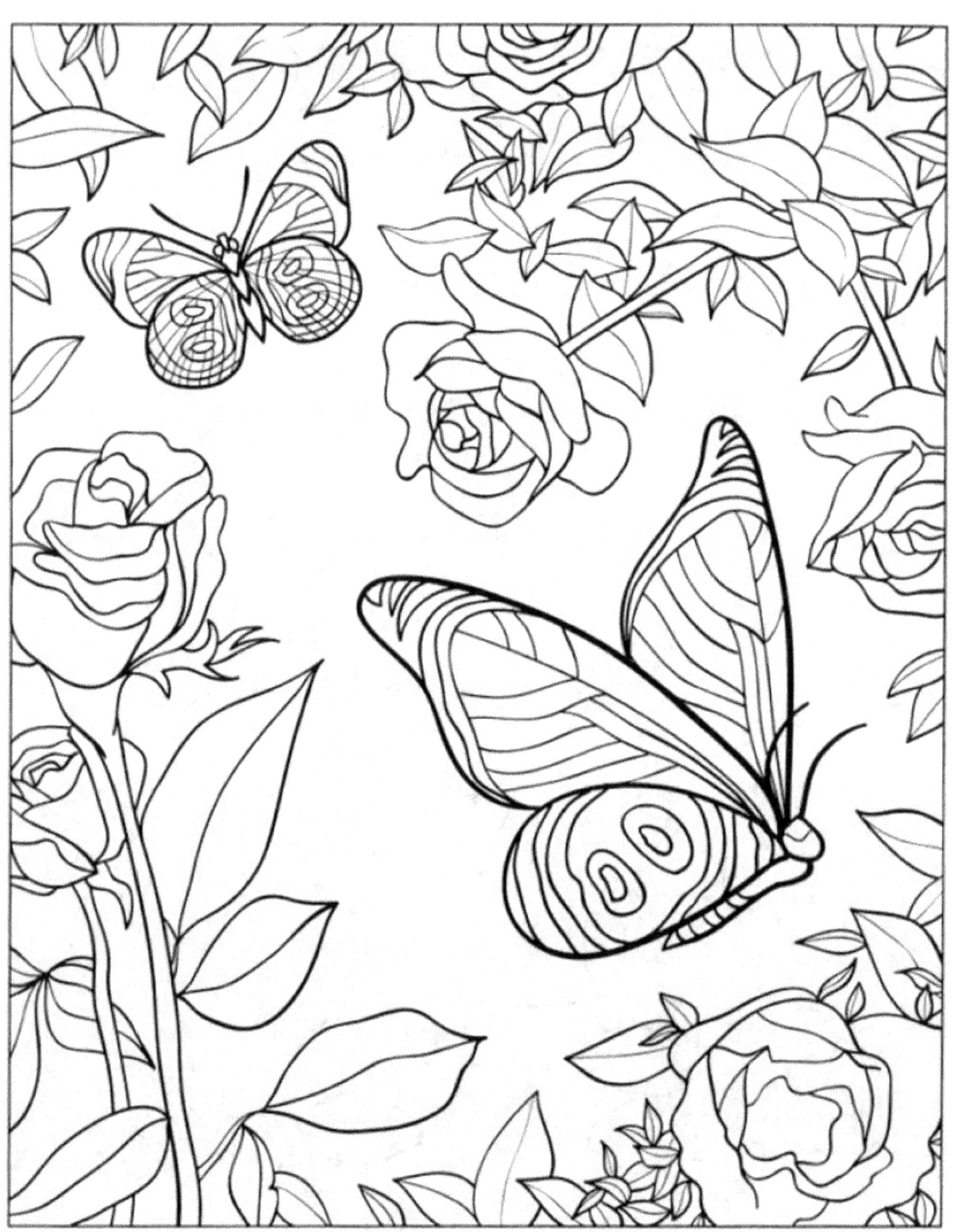

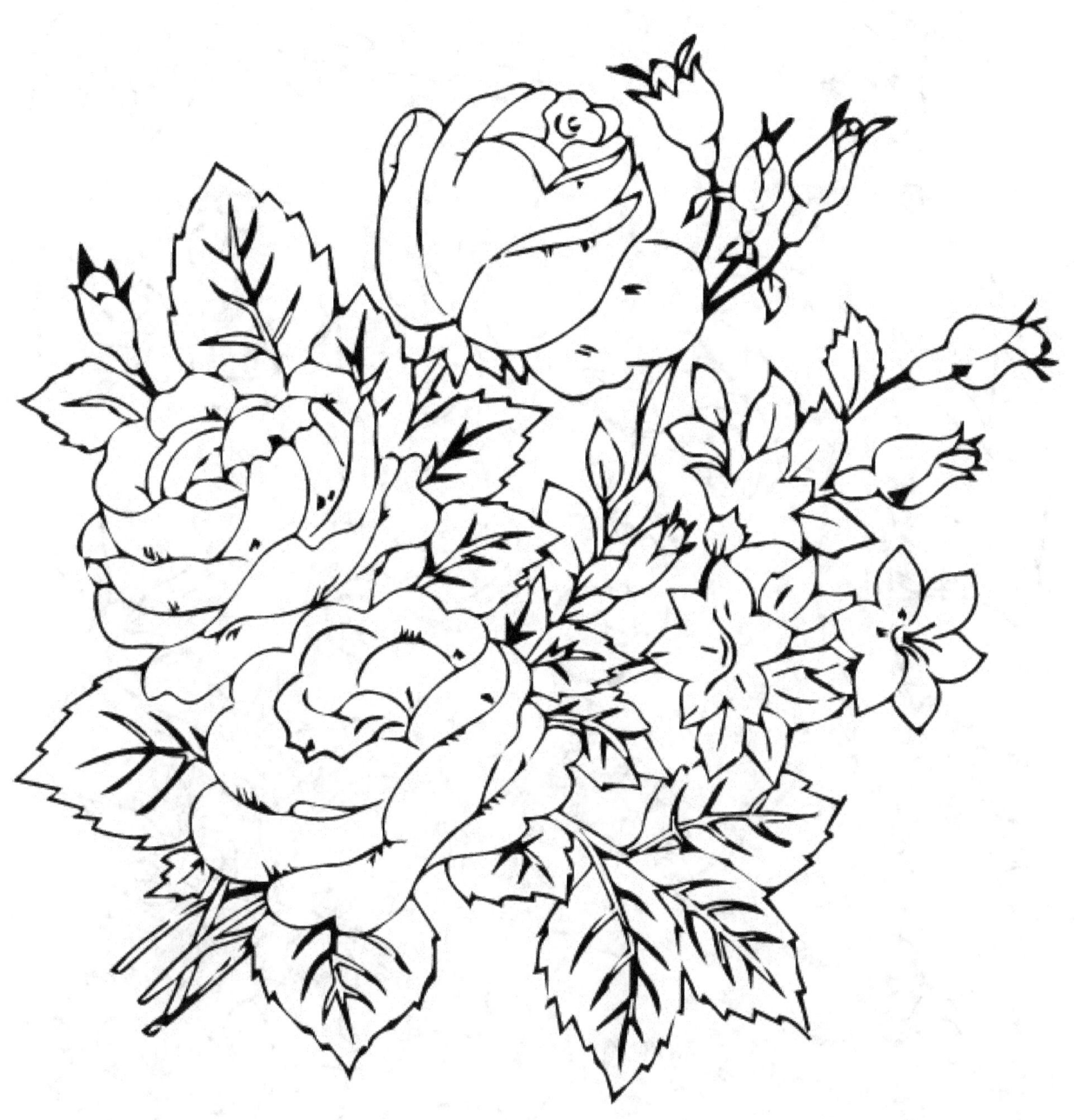

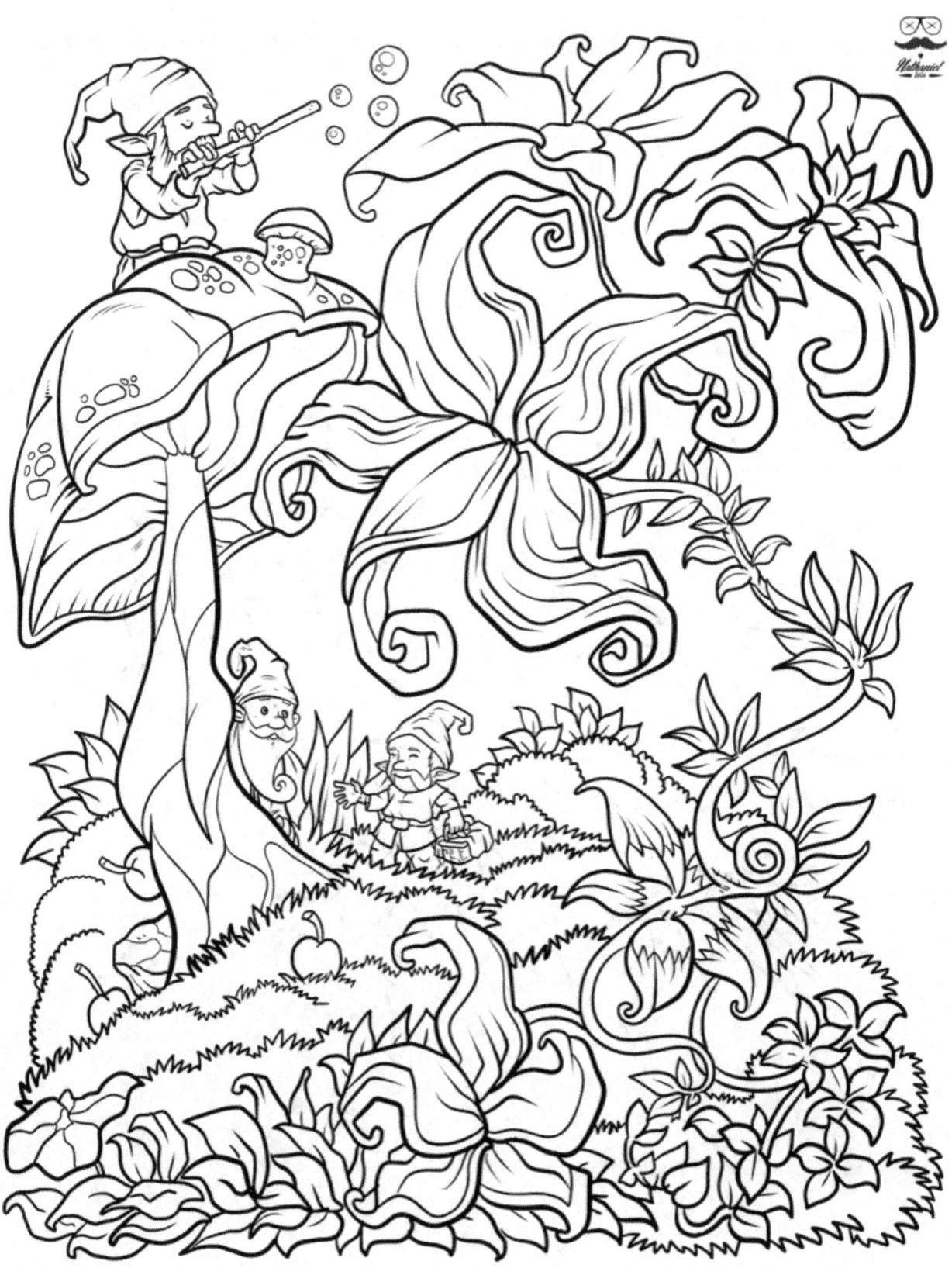

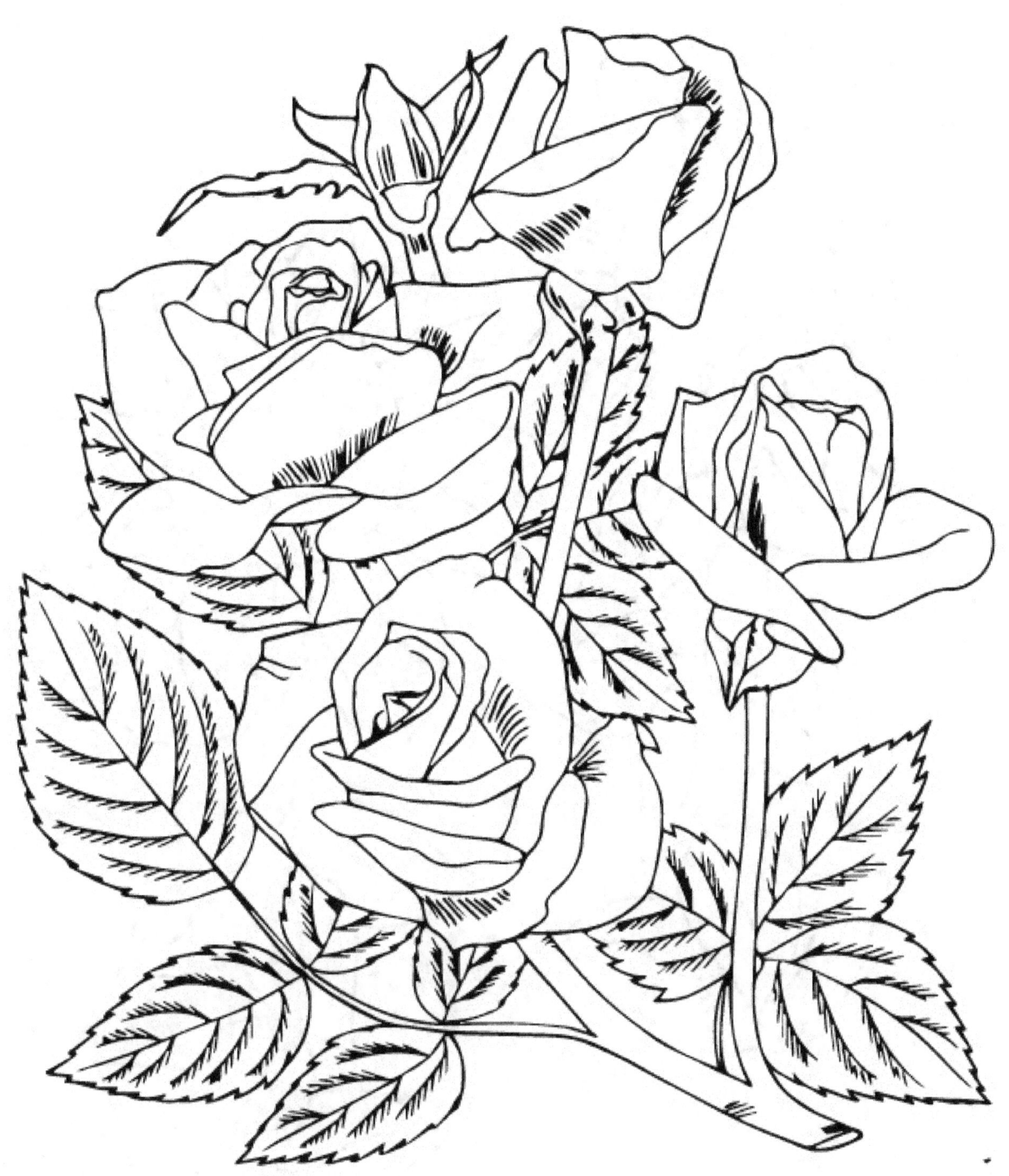

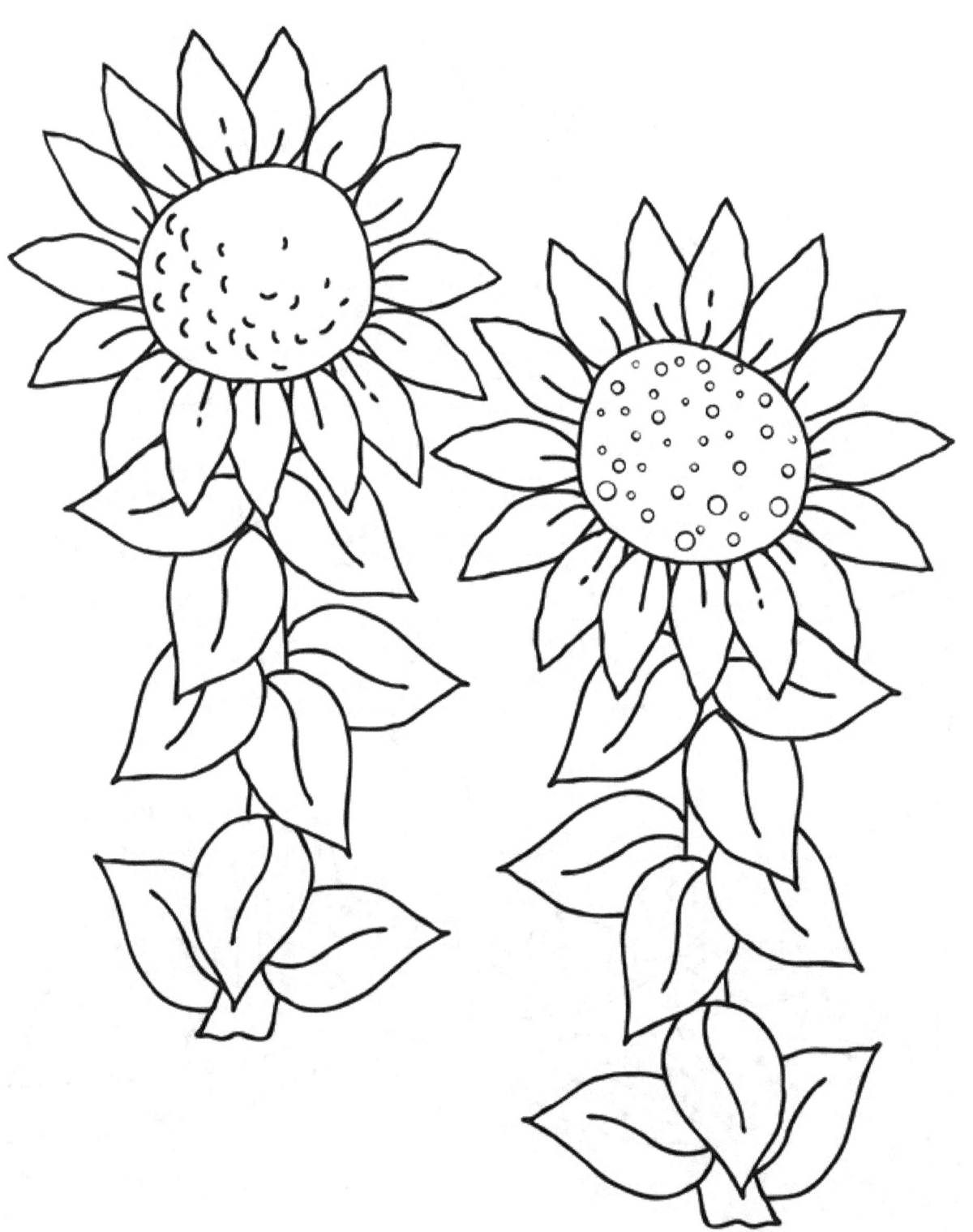

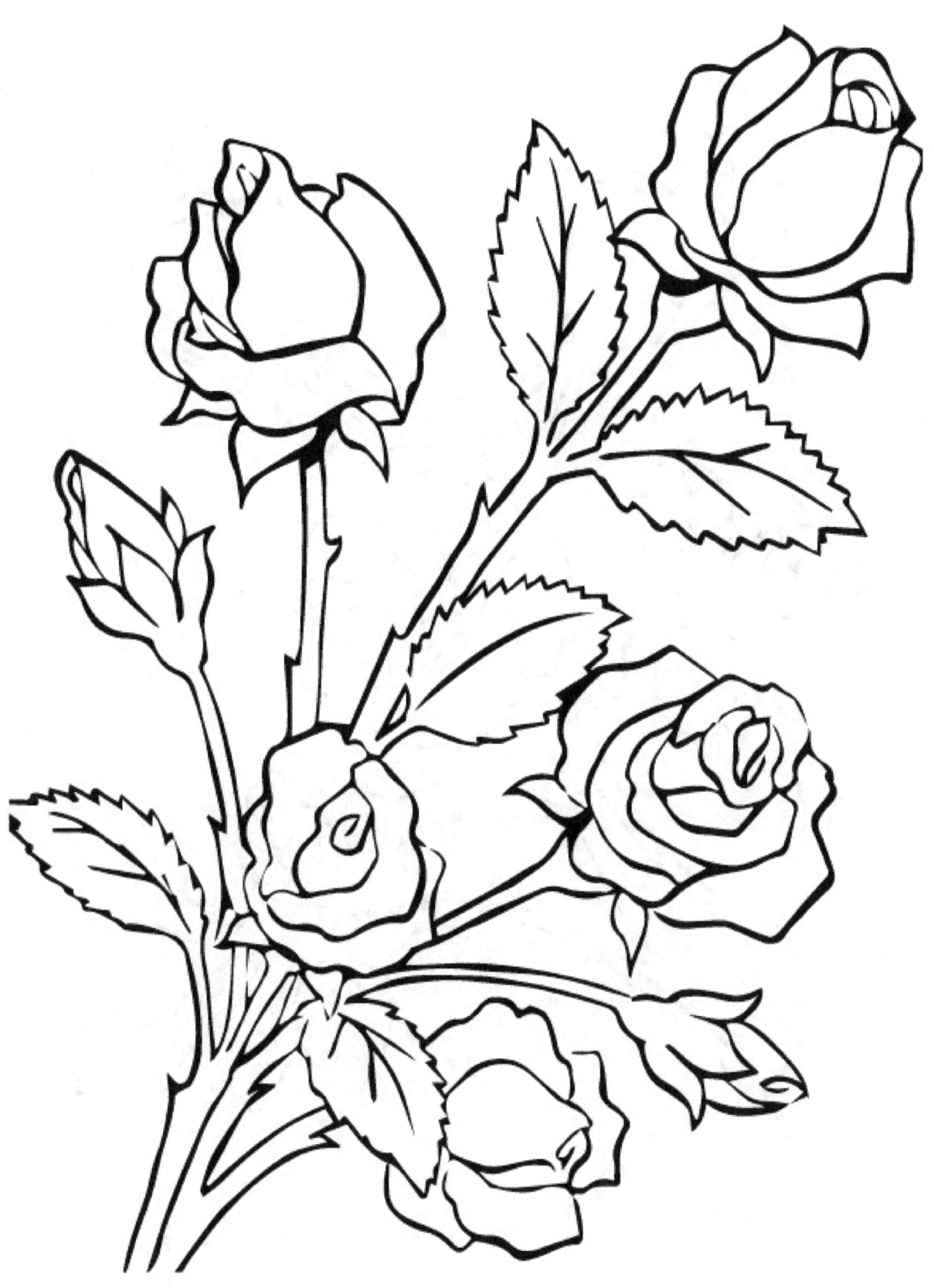

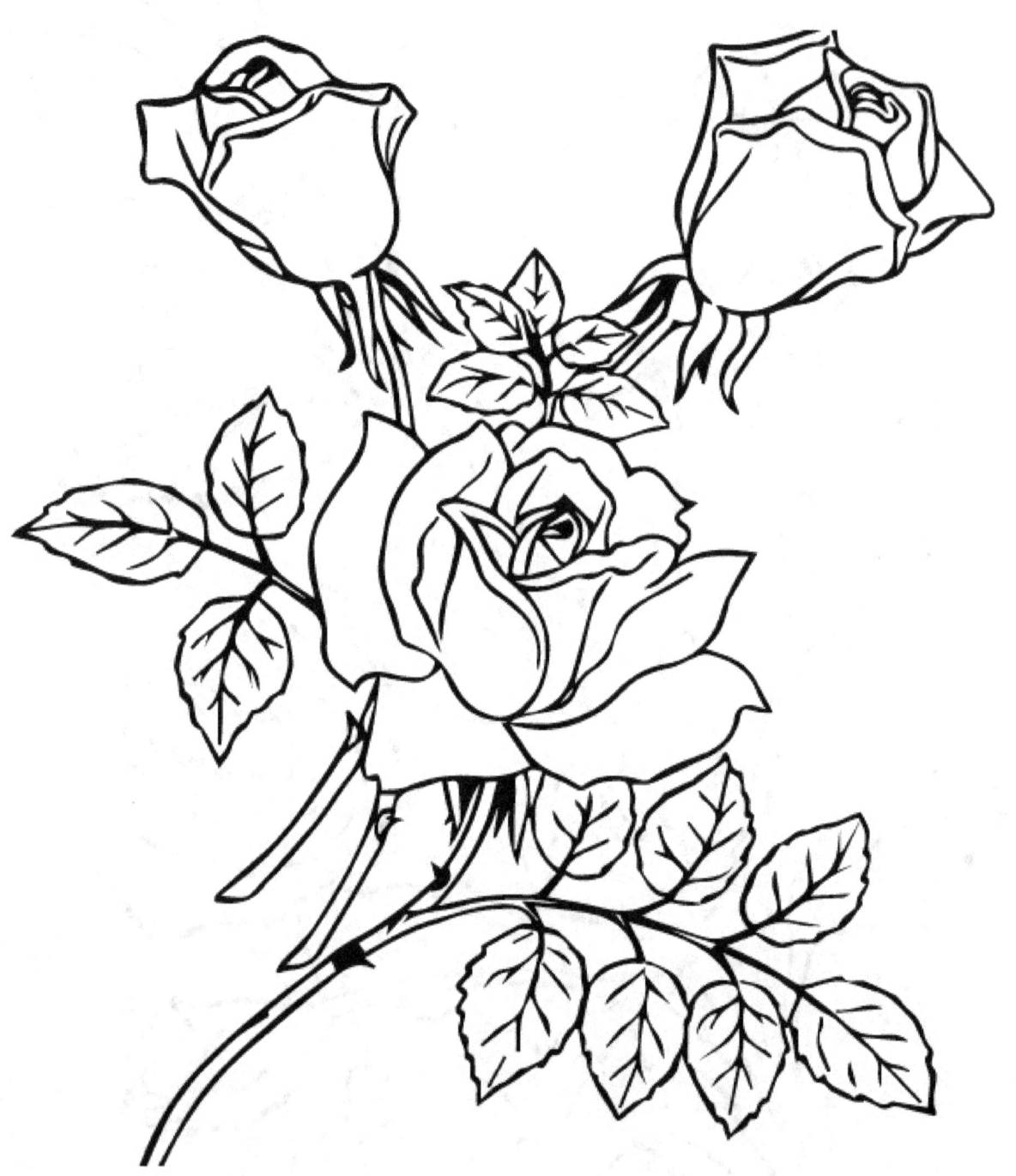

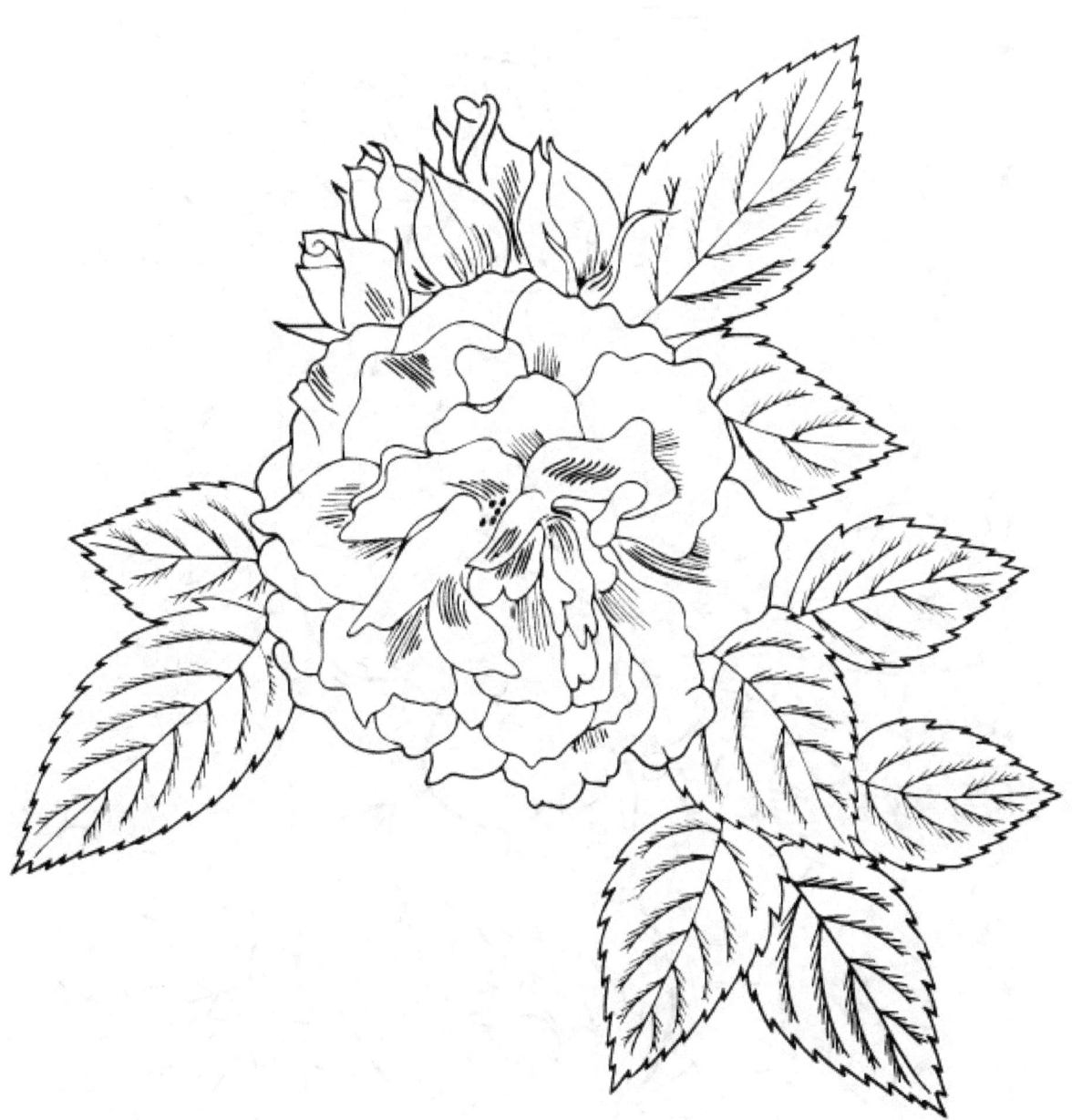

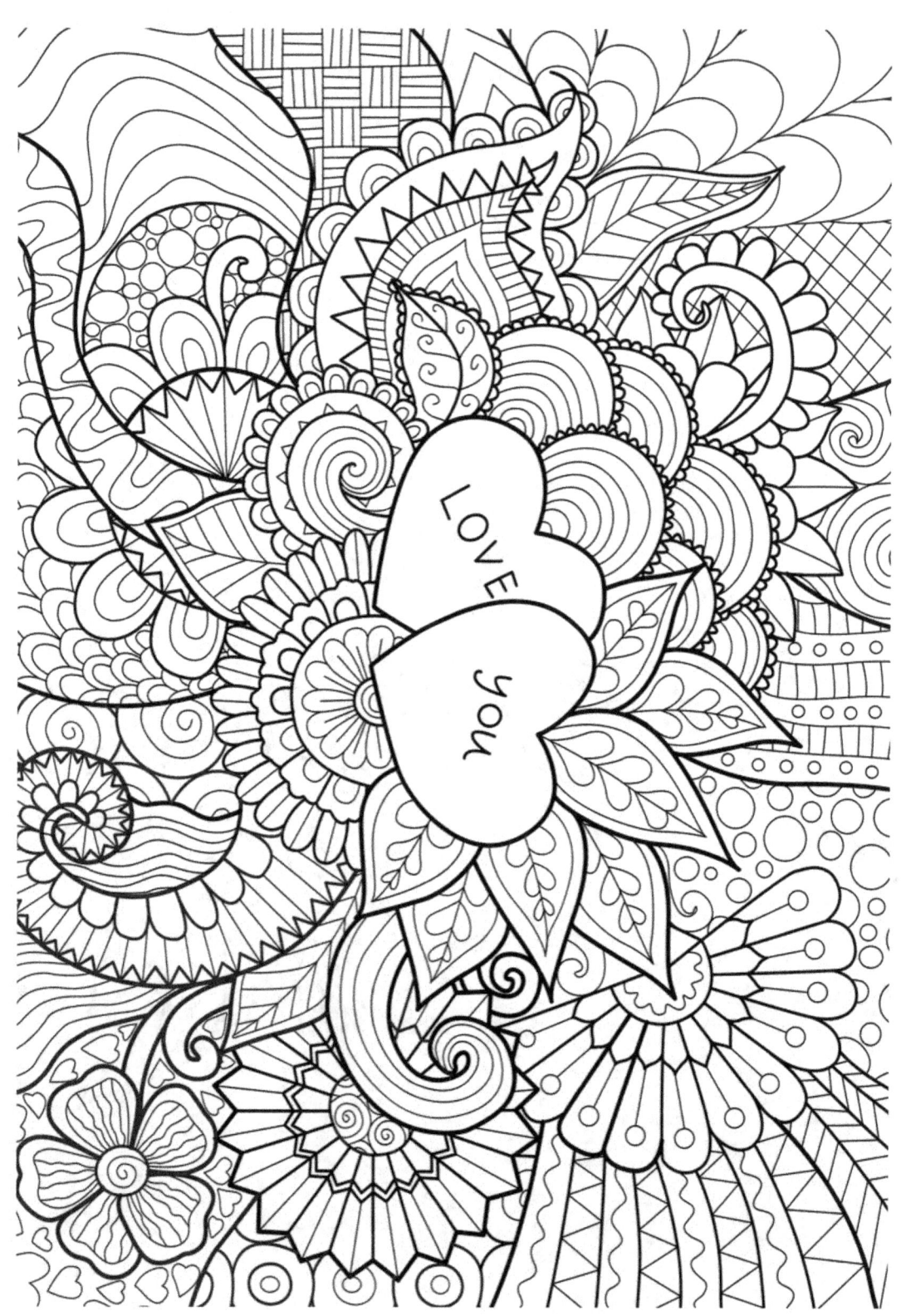

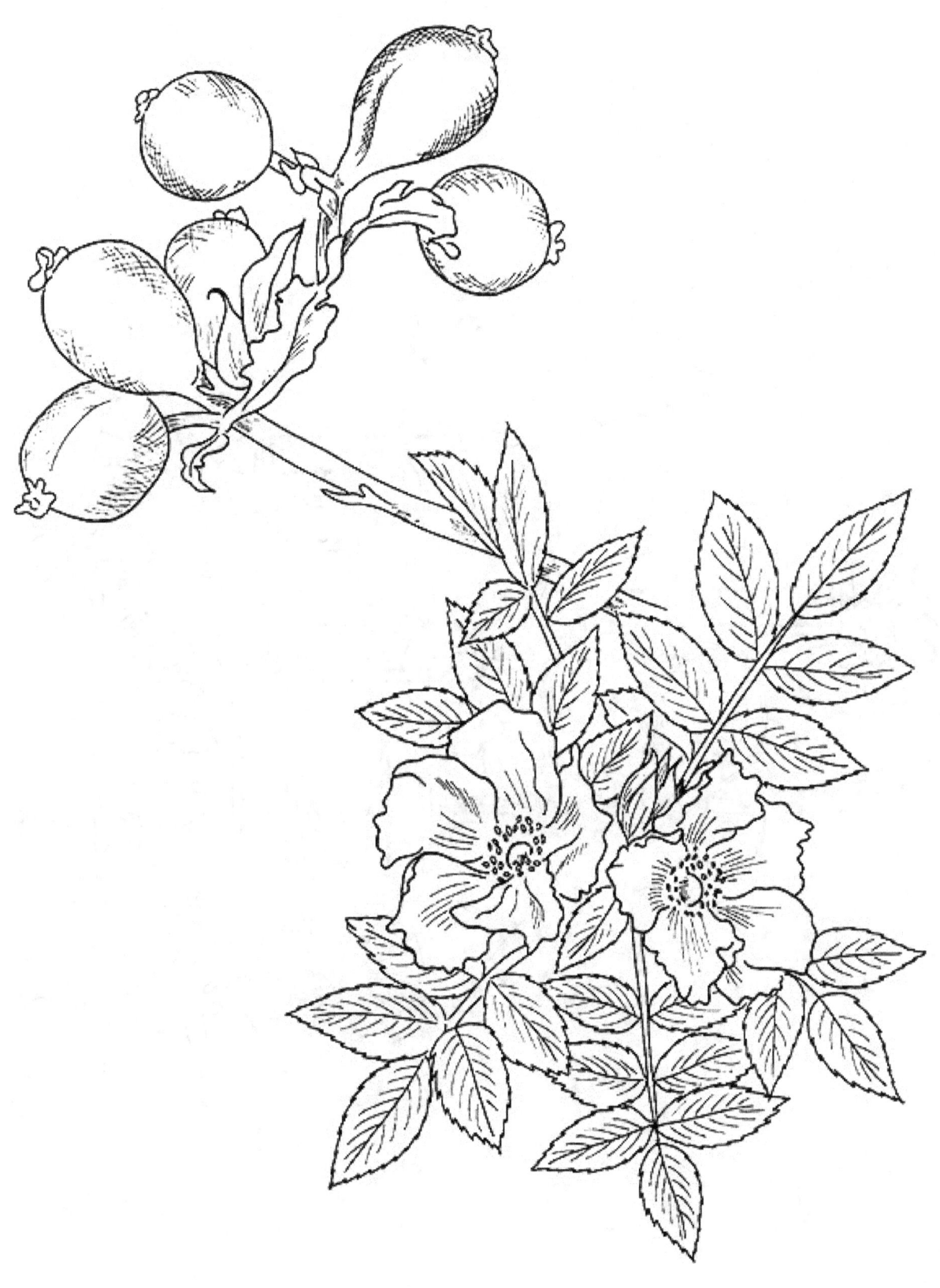

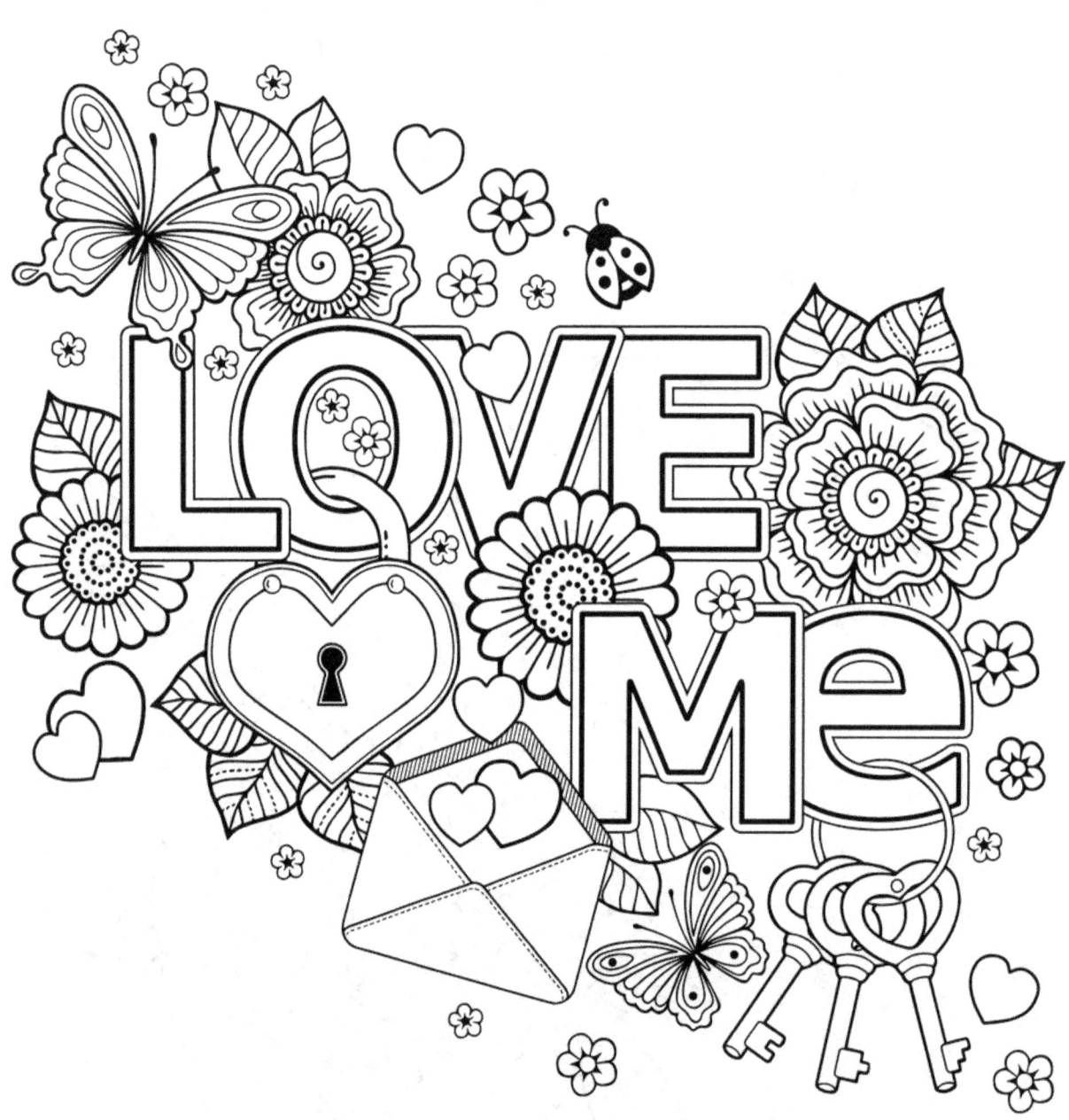

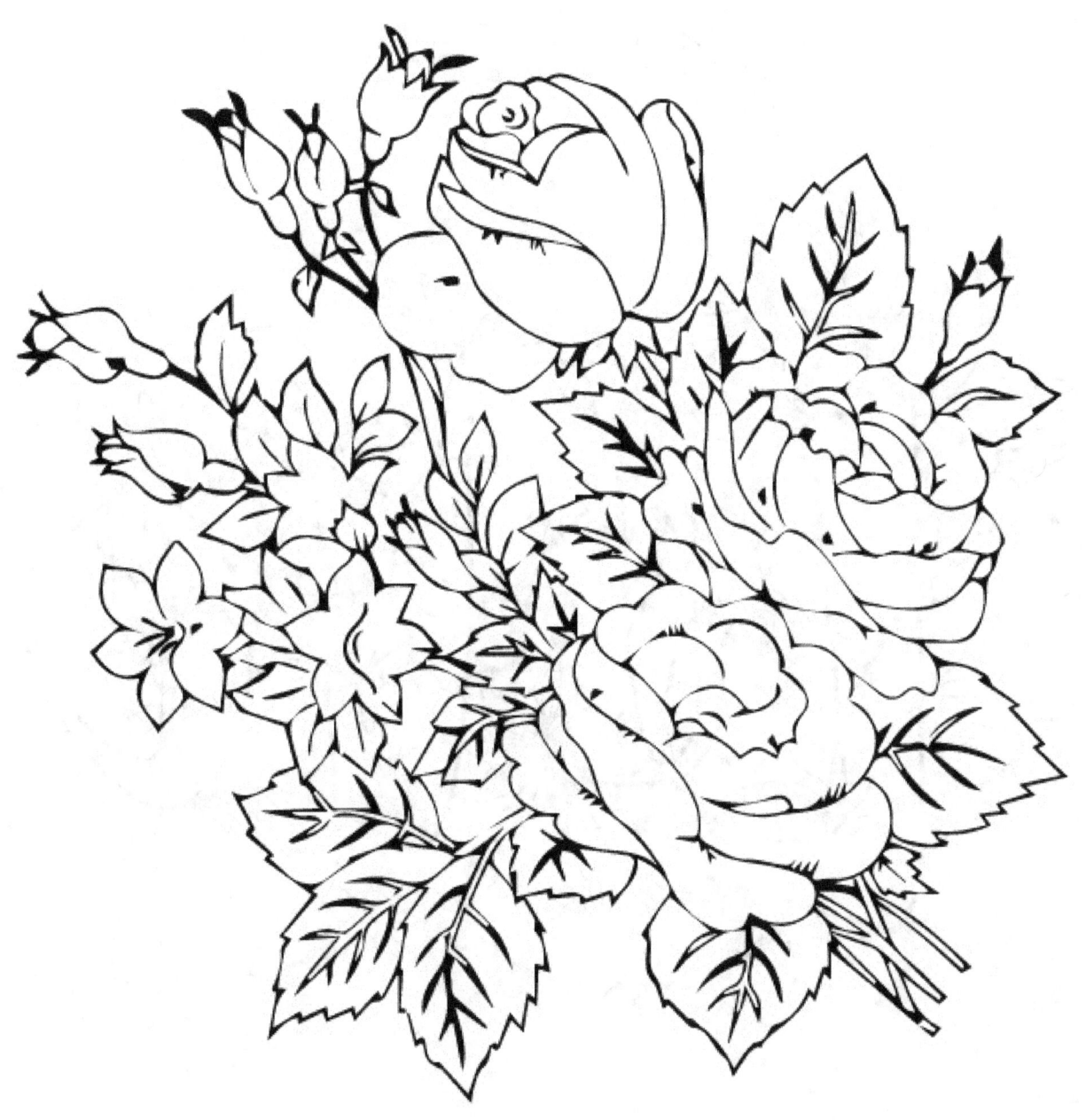

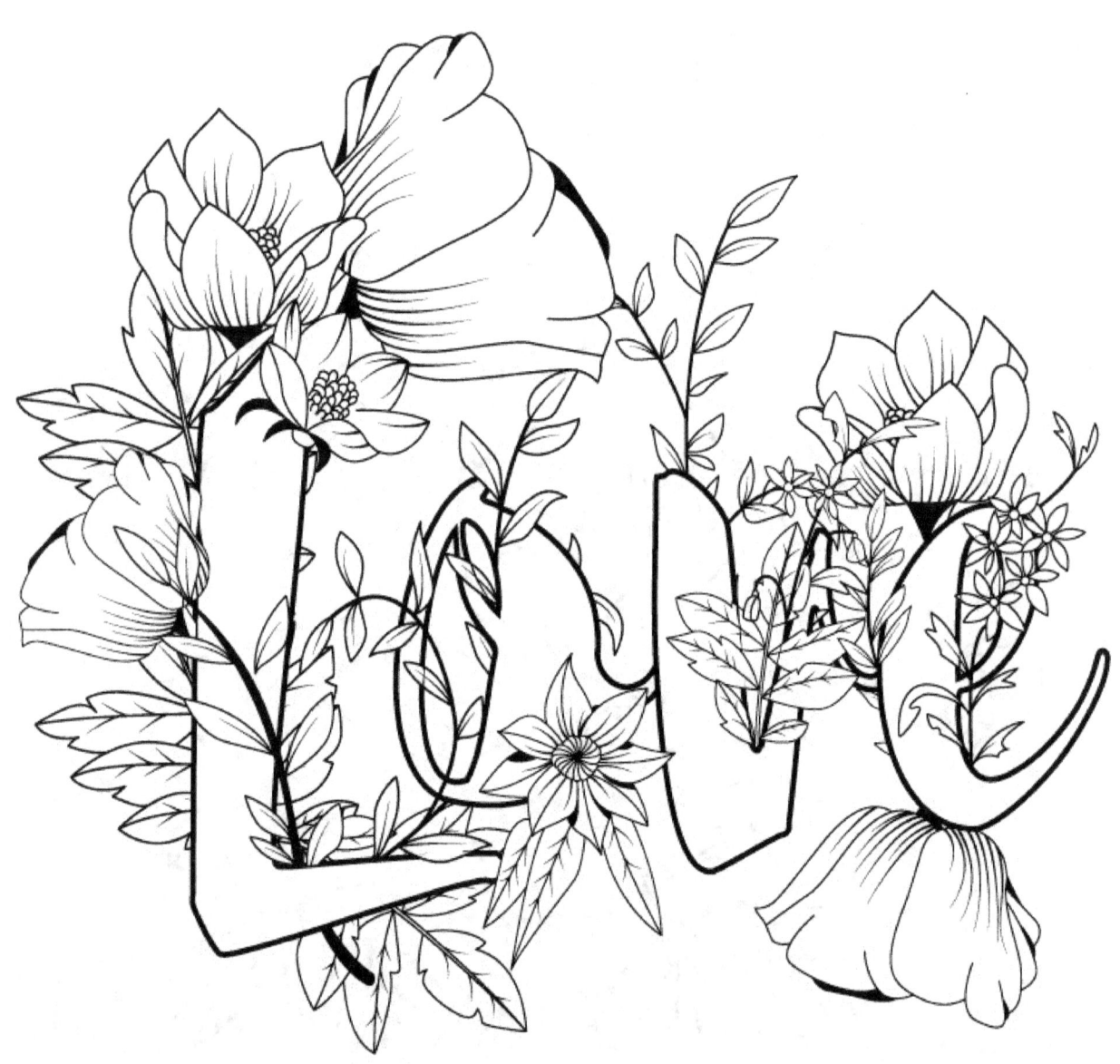

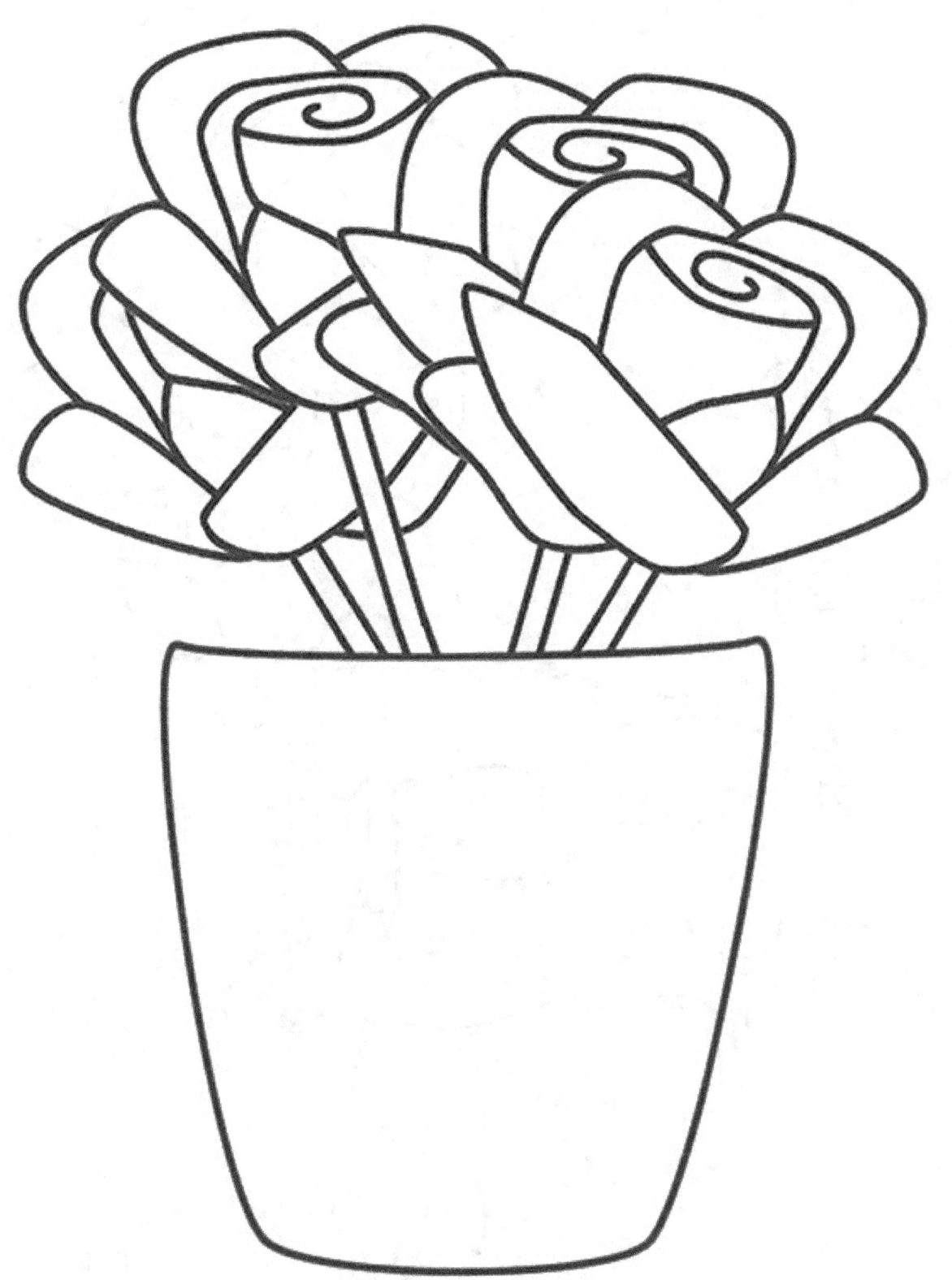

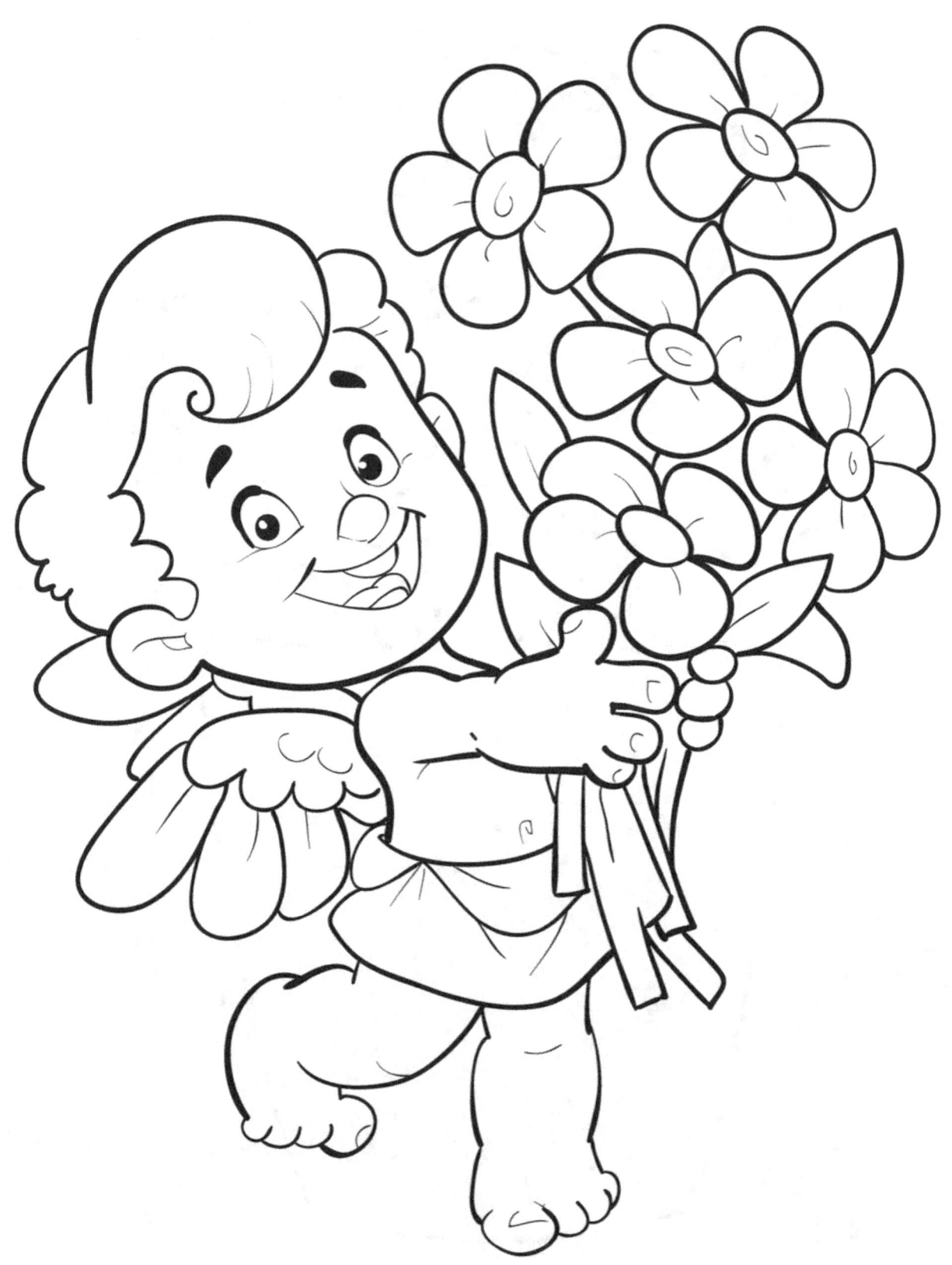

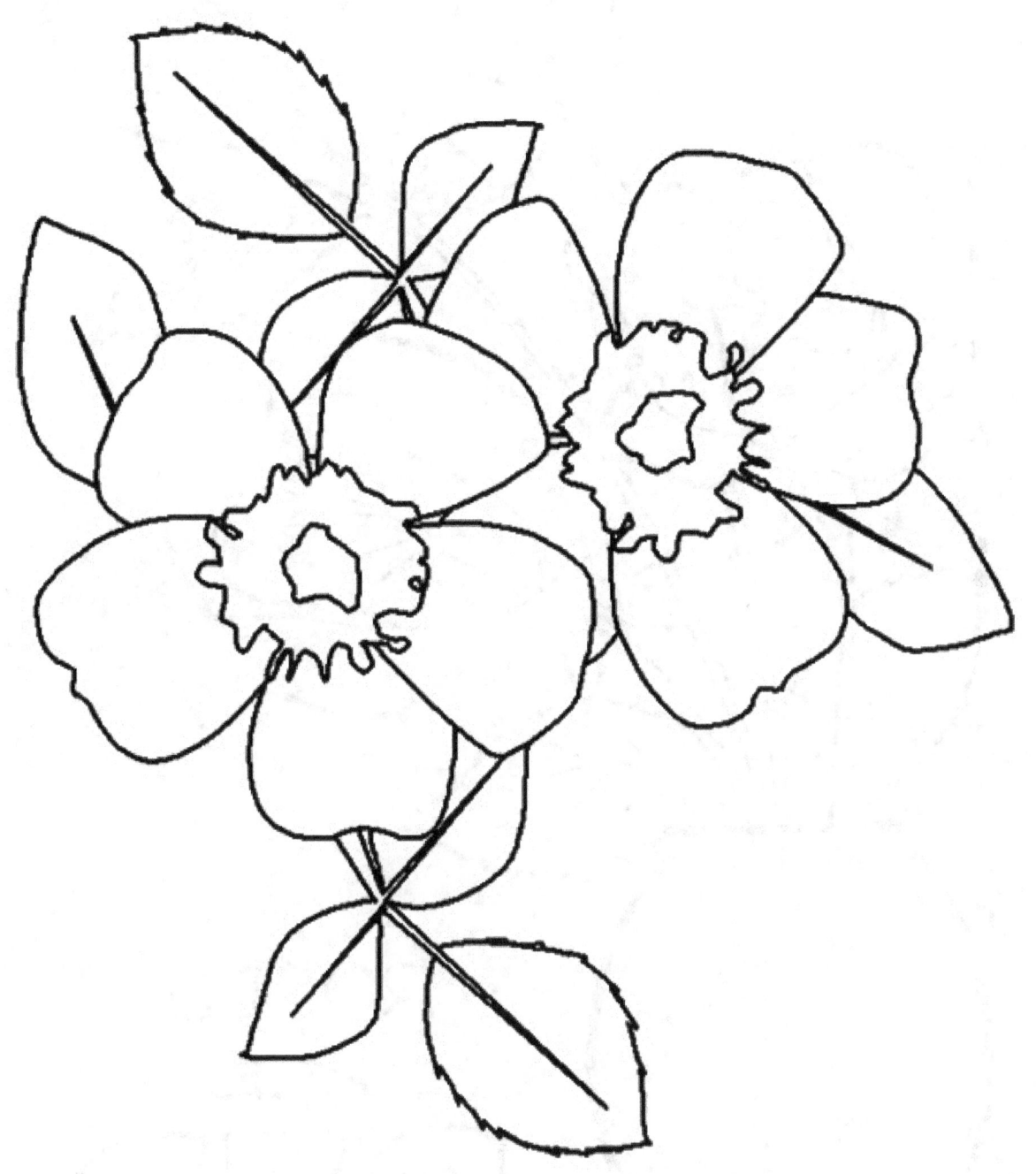

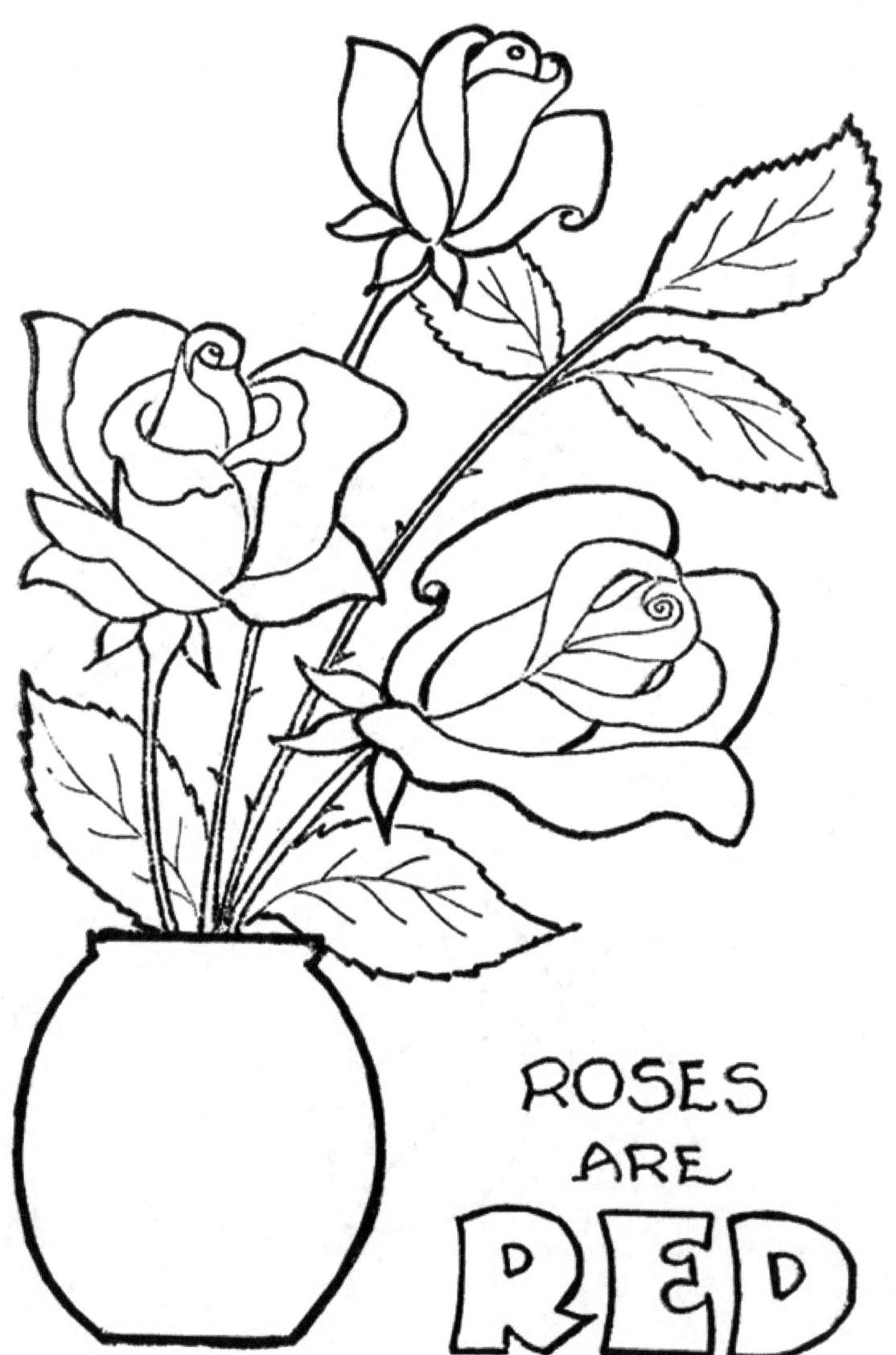

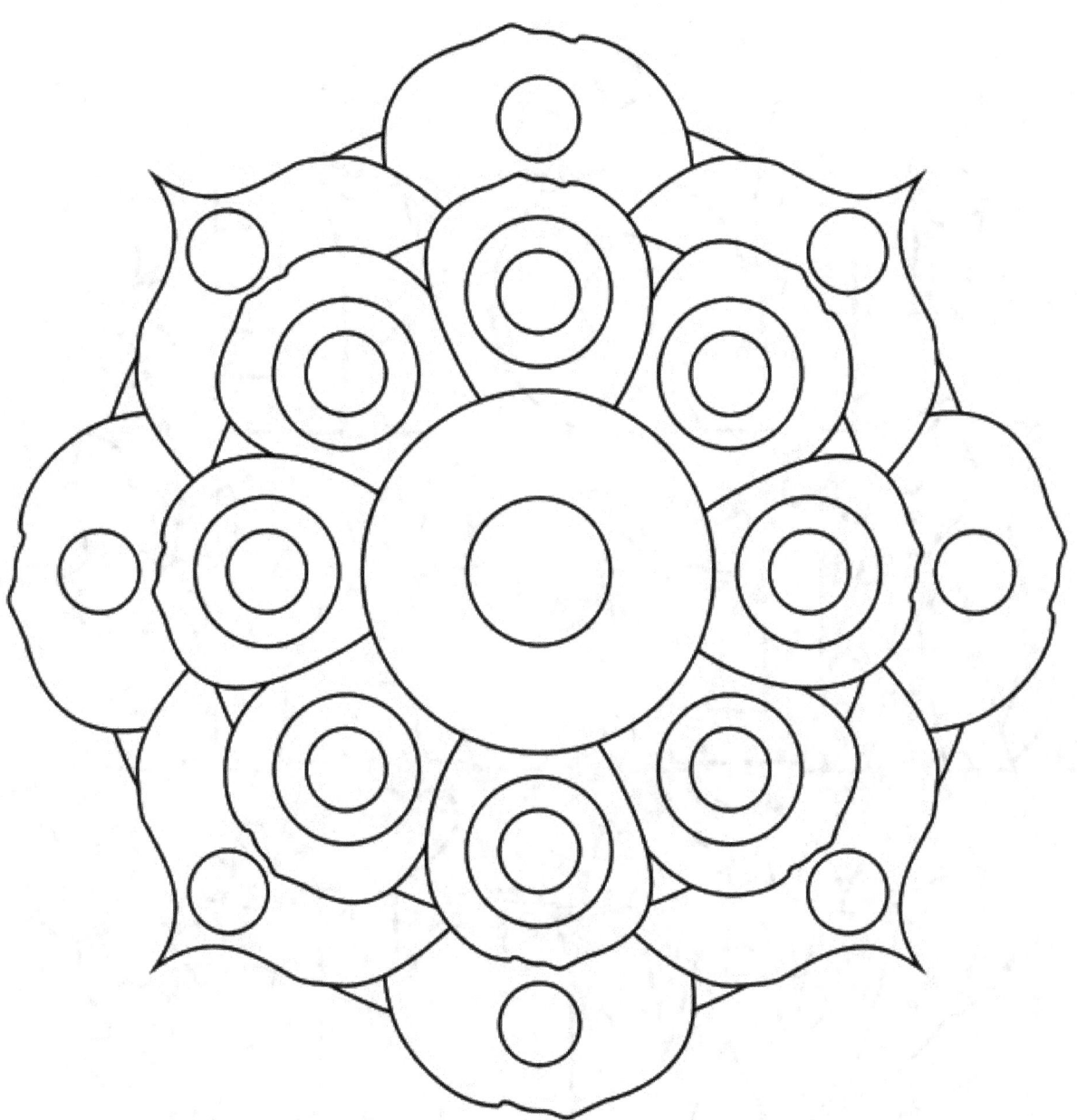

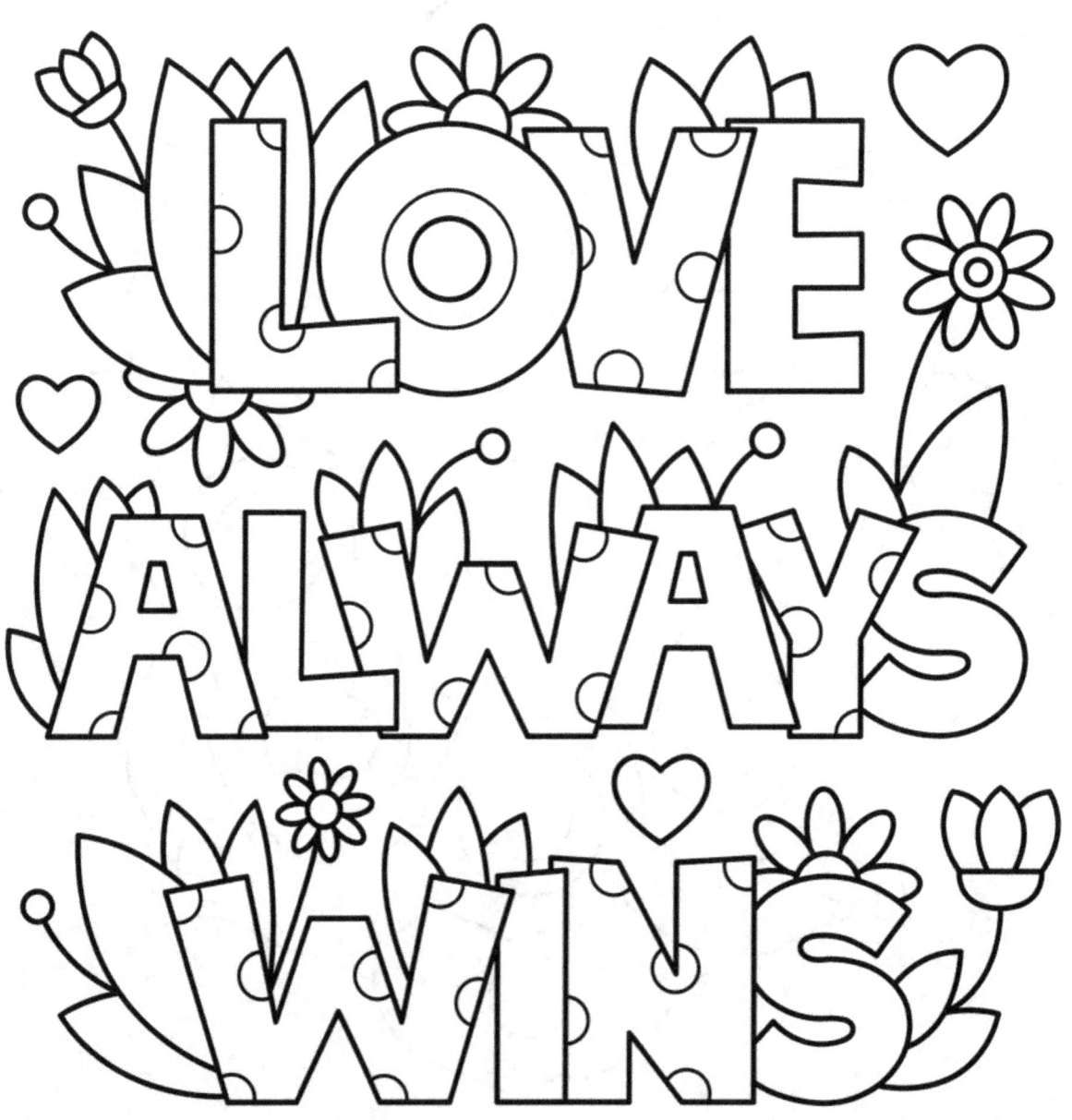

www.ingramcontent.com/pod-product-compliance
Lightning Source LLC
Chambersburg PA
CBHW060427220526
45465CB00008B/3048